BACKPAC

THE OUTDOORS AT YOUR DOORSTEP

Tent and Car Camper's Handbook

BACKPACKER

THE OUTDOORS AT YOUR DOORSTEP

Tent and Car Camper's Handbook

ADVICE FOR FAMILIES & FIRST-TIMERS

Buck Tilton, M.S.
with Kristin Hostetter

THE MOUNTAINEERS BOOKS

THE MOUNTAINEERS BOOKS
*is the nonprofit publishing arm of The Mountaineers Club, an organization
founded in 1906 and dedicated to the exploration, preservation, and
enjoyment of outdoor and wilderness areas.*

1001 SW Klickitat Way, Suite 201, Seattle, WA 98134

BACKPACKER
THE OUTDOORS AT YOUR DOORSTEP
33 East Minor Street
Emmaus, PA 18098

Distributed in the United Kingdom by Cordee, www.cordee.co.uk

Manufactured in the United States of America

Acquiring Editor: Cassandra Conyers
Project Editor: Mary Metz
Copy Editor: Heath Lynn Silberfeld/Enough Said
Cover and Book Design: The Mountaineers Books
Layout: Mayumi Thompson
Illustrator: Brian Metz/Green Rhino Graphics and Hans Neuhart/Electronic Illustrators Group

Front cover photo: © Corbis/Royalty Free
Back cover photo: courtesy of Johnson Outdoors, Inc.

Library of Congress Cataloging-in-Publication Data
Tilton, Buck.
  Tent and car camper's handbook : advice for families & first-timers /
Buck Tilton.
     p. cm.
  Includes index.
  ISBN 1-59485-011-9
  1. Camping. 2. Survival skills. I. Title: Tent and car camper's
handbook. II. Title.
  GV191.7.T56 2006
  796.54—dc22
                                         2005035055

♻ Printed on recycled paper
ISBN (paperback): 978-1-59485-011-0
ISBN (ebook): 978-1-59485-241-1

CONTENTS

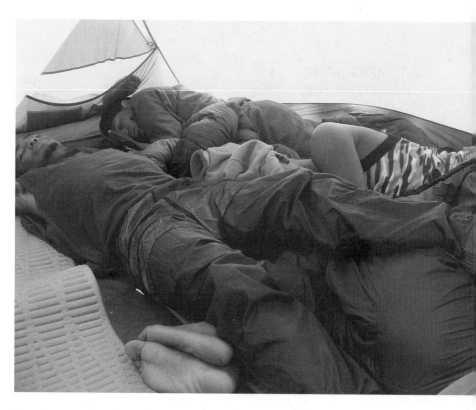

Sometimes camping nirvana is a mid-afternoon snooze.

FOREWORD

A s I write this, my husband is out in the driveway unloading the gear from our weekend camping trip in Vermont. My two boys, five-year-old Charlie and three-year-old Joey, have beelined upstairs to the playroom and are in the midst of erecting a "tent" made of sofa cushions and blankets. They have headlamps strapped to their little blonde noggins, copious amounts of dirt under their fingernails, a few bug bites, and tee shirts that smell like campfire. The bathtub will have to wait.

Camping brings out the kid in all of us. There's something magical about sleeping in a tent. Set one up in the living room on a rainy day and you have an instant "fort." Pitch one in the woods and call it home for a couple of nights: that's pure heaven.

It's hard for me to articulate the real, true, big-picture reason I love camping. Sure, it's partly the wonderful sights, sounds, and smells. It's also the feeling of escaping into a simpler world. Really, though, it's a combination of a thousand tiny things: like hearing raindrops on my tent fly and knowing I'm snug and dry inside, like the exquisite taste of a chunk of sharp Cheddar coupled with a slice of spicy salami and a dollop of mustard, like the way my skin tingles when I plunge into an icy mountain lake.

This book is a must read for a few types of people. If you've never set foot in a campground but want to test the waters, you'll find tips on what to pack, where and when to go, and how to set up a tent. In a nutshell, everything you need to get started.

For those of us who have many "grown-up" adventures under our belts but now find ourselves in the family way, this guide offers advice on how to keep our kids safe, comfortable, and enthralled with the camping experience.

If you're a longtime occasional camper who simply wants to make your time outside more enjoyable, you'll find tips on cooking impressive meals, sleeping more comfortably, and staying dry.

This book is brimming with hands-on information that was learned the hard way. Take for example a story Buck Tilton, the author, told me once: "A long time ago, as a relative newby, I set my tent on an exceptionally lovely and flat spot, with a great view of a nearby lake. Trouble was, it rained cats and dogs all night, and the flat spot was also the lowest spot for probably a mile in all directions. By the time I abandoned the tent, the floor was under several inches of water." Woops! The good news is that, after reading this book, you won't make a similar mistake. In fact, you'll be well equipped to experience camping nirvana.

It might hit you when you poke your head out of your tent one dawn and find a deer tiptoeing through your campsite. Maybe it will happen one night as you watch your son's s'more-smeared, smiling face in the flickering light of the campfire. It could happen in a thousand different ways.

Trust me, camping nirvana will happen to you. And you'll know it when you feel it. All you have to do is go camping!

Happy trails,
Kristin Hostetter
Gear Editor, *Backpacker Magazine*
August 2005

INTRODUCTION

Because you're holding this book in your hands, you've been thinking about going camping. Even if you've already logged a few nights in the outdoors, you're thinking about more. You're thinking about it because you desire, and maybe need, a real change of pace. You imagine, or you know, the peace of open spaces, the unhurried beauty of wild land, the brush of a breeze tainted with pine sap and wildflowers, the anticipation of quality time with family and friends, and the bright colors of sunset reflected in a still lake. It's all there, and much more, and you cannot experience it to the fullest until you set camp in the middle of it—and you're holding the right book to get started and to get beyond the basics.

{ In the Words of a Sage }

I went to the woods because I wished to live deliberately, to confront only the essential facts of life, and see if I could not learn what it had to teach, and not, when I came to die, discover that I had not lived.

—*Henry David Thoreau*

As far as this book is concerned, camping occurs most often in a state or national campground, although we'll briefly visit setting camp in a remote site. There can be, if you choose, fresh water, rest rooms, fire grates, even showers and laundry rooms. There will be attractions: things to see (a visitor center, a nature trail, historical sites) and things to do (hiking, swimming, boating, fishing, biking) a short distance away. But you'll awake each morning and return each afternoon to an established campsite.

Approximately 72 percent of camping trips involve families.

{ Personal Reflections }

On my hard cot, olive drab in color, I rolled over in my stuffy sleeping bag, olive drab in color, and listened to the heavy canvas of the tent wall, olive drab in color, flapping noisily in a stiff breeze off the dark lake. My dad was still active military, and olive drab, military issue, was the color of our camp. Other camps near and far, across the state and across the nation, though few in number, reflected the same drab tones. If you pressed me for a specific day, or month, or even the year of that night—my first tent camping experience—I'd be unable to answer. I can tell you it was nearly five decades ago, and I can tell you anyone looking for camping gear ended up at a military surplus store. We postwar baby boomers were still—well—babies, the soon-to-be flood of outdoor enthusiasts was a mere trickle, and you couldn't find much camping stuff except in stores that sold what the United States Army and Navy had manufactured and then found they had in relatively enormous excess.

Dinner had been the catch-of-the-day, fried in a large and very heavy cast-iron skillet over the coals of a fire. Lightweight cooking gear was to appear years later, and a camping stove was not part of our arsenal. When it got dark, it stayed dark. We didn't have a lantern. Before bedtime, against the chill of the night, I donned a scratchy wool sweater, struggling to get it over a flannel shirt. Synthetic clothing was a thing of the future. When I stepped away from the cot, I stood on dirt. Tents with floors were not available.

All those memories are important to me, but they are incidental to one critical point: I was enthralled. The outdoors, in some still indefinable way, touched my mind, my heart, my soul. I loved the warmth of the crackling fire, stuffing my soiled feet into the sleeping bag, inhaling the weed-soaked air, and fearing the darkness. A seed was planted that sprouted into a lifelong yearning to return again and again. I have nurtured the sprout, setting up camp too many times to remember: in mountain valleys, beneath towering trees, on sandy desert floors, not far from the tidal surge of beaches, near the damp banks of blackwater swamps. And I will keep returning, again and again, almost always now with my wife, as often as possible with my children. Camping is inseparable from the person I am, a large part of who we are as a family. To risk being overly dramatic, the camping experience is something we cherish beyond words—and I like thinking it will become the same experience for you.

Just the Facts: Millions Are Camping

In 2000, 42.2 million Americans camped out at least once.

In 2003, 53 million Americans camped out at least once.

In 2003, more than 51 million Americans took more than one camping trip.

In 2004, one out of every four Americans participated in an outdoor adventure—primarily hiking, swimming, fishing—and camping.

U.S. campers are currently 54 percent male and 46 percent female.

About 42 percent of campers go with a spouse or significant other.

Approximately 72 percent of camping trips involve families.

Camping is the seventh most popular recreational activity in the United States.

—From the Sporting Goods Manufacturers Association and the Outdoor Industry Association.

TECHNO: THE OLD VERSUS THE NEW

	The Old	The New
Campsite	Dirt and rocks	Well-managed sites, amazing amenities
Tents	Heavy, cumbersome, floorless	Lightweight, easy setup, protective
Bags	Something to try to sleep in	An irresistible, restful bed
Kitchen	Campfire	Fast and efficient stoves
Clothing	Heavy, scratchy, drab	Light, comfortable, colorful

If your outdoor experiences have been limited to grilling on the back deck, you'll be ready to gather and pack the essentials—and a few luxuries—after absorbing this book. You'll learn about picking the best spot, setting camp, cooking, getting involved in activities in and around camp, providing first aid if needed, and more. Even if you've bagged more than a few nights out, you'll find your knowledge expanded—and your camping skills improved. You'll be ready to minimize the fuss and maximize the fun.

A Note About Safety

Safety is an important concern in all outdoor activities. No book can alert you to every hazard or anticipate the limitations of every reader. The descriptions of techniques and procedures in this book are intended to provide general information. This is not a complete text on camping technique. Nothing substitutes for formal instruction, routine practice, and plenty of experience. When you follow any of the procedures described here, you assume responsibility for your own safety. Use this book as a general guide to further information. Under normal conditions, excursions into the backcountry require attention to traffic, road and trail conditions, weather, terrain, the capabilities of your party, and other factors. Keeping informed on current conditions and exercising common sense are the keys to a safe, enjoyable outing.

—*The Mountaineers Books*

2

GETTING READY

In the driveway, or in the garage, the vehicle sits. Miles away, the campsite waits. When the two—vehicle and campsite—meet, you'll be unpacking a pile of gear and clothing: all you need to live outdoors. At home you don't think often about what you *really* need. It's there, in the cupboard, on a shelf, in the refrigerator, or down the street at the market. But when you pack for a camping trip, you *do* have to consider thoughtfully everything you might want to have with you. That's what this chapter is about.

{ In the Words of a Sage }

For me, and for thousands with similar inclinations, the most important passion of life is the overpowering desire to escape periodically from the clutches of a mechanistic civilization.

—*Bob Marshall*

Yes, the camping experience is something of a gear-intensive experience. You need at least the basic stuff, or you're not going camping, but you can have a great time with remarkably little—a sort of "low-intensity" camping—or you can attempt to recreate your home—more of a "high-intensity" camping experience. The choices are yours to make. The important rooms in your home will be represented: the bedroom, the kitchen, the bathroom—but no hard and fast rules govern what to take. The guidelines will even change a little to match your specific camping destination and situation. Where are you going: the desert, the seashore, the mountains? At what time of year? How many people will be with you? Perhaps an even more significant question to answer is this: how technological do you want to be? You'll have to decide, and this chapter will help you.

Just the Facts: Camping "Intensity" Comparison Chart		
Low "Intensity"	**Medium "Intensity"**	**High "Intensity"**
small tent	large tent	very large tent
sleeping bags	sleeping bags	sleeping bags
sleeping pads	sleeping pads	sleeping pads and cots
cold food	small stove	large stove
flashlight	pots and pan	pots and pans
	cooler of food	Dutch oven
	camp chairs	griddle
	lantern	portable kitchen ensemble
		camp chairs
		camp table
		portable toilet
		lanterns
		flashlights
		saw, shovel, hatchet

Be warned: most people, after a camping trip or two, get hooked. Once hooked, you'll want more and more of your own stuff. Some of it you already own. You'll find items you use around the house that can be used on a camping trip or adapted to camping use, such as pots and pans. Some gear you'll need to purchase, your tent being one example and your sleeping bags being another. If you suddenly feel your finances threatened, relax. Yes, you can spend a lot if you want, but you'll be pleasantly surprised by how little money it takes for a careful shopper to get completely set up for splendid camping. You'll find some shopping advice in this chapter, too.

BORROW OR RENT: Borrow camping gear. Save that trip to an outdoor specialty store or discount house until you've logged a few days of experience. If you can't borrow, rent. Outfitting services will happily and inexpensively provide everything you'll need. You need a *feel* for what you want before you lay down cash for what you want.

SHOPPING TIME: The best bargains on camping gear are typically available in the fall. I've seen, for example, a Coleman Family Camping Package for less than $200. It contained a four-person tent, two sleeping bags, two camp chairs, a lantern, a grill, a half-gallon jug, a small ax, and a storage container. Some great deals can be found year-round, such as L. L. Bean's Discovery Camping set: a tent, sleeping pad, sleeping bag, and camp pillow for about $159.

BRAND NAMES: This book mentions gear, now and then, by brand name—just to give you a sample of what is being discussed. In every category, you'll find many excellent brands from numerous reputable manufacturers. The choices you make should always be *your* choices.

The Tent

A tent is not *truly* your home away from home, but it's at least a place to sleep and, perhaps, a reading room or playroom. Numerous styles of tents are available. The one you choose should meet the demands you'll place on it: the demands of the season, the environment, and the people who will use it.

Characteristics of Every Good Tent

1. *You need a tent that stays dry inside—no matter what's happening outside.* Today almost all tents are manufactured with thin, strong nylon, but not all the nylon is made the same. The nylon of the floor of a tent must be waterproof, allowing no moisture to soak through from the ground. Tent floors are made of material more durable than the rest of the tent, and they should extend at least a few inches up the walls of a tent if you want to keep all ground moisture and splattering rain from soaking through. The part of the tent exposed directly to rain, and to rain propelled slantwise by a high wind, also must be waterproof. In some styles, the tent itself will be waterproof. More often than not, the tent walls and roof are not waterproof, but the tent comes with a waterproof fly, a separate piece of nylon that is set up over the tent using the same poles that hold the tent erect. With all tents, a rain fly provides better protection than a waterproof tent because it allows ventilation between the tent walls and the fly, reducing or entirely preventing condensation inside the tent.
2. *You need a tent with good ventilation.* A tent must have enough openings—vents—in the form of doors and windows to allow air to pass through. Without ventilation, even when the air is dry, sleepers alone will release enough moisture to dampen the inside of a tent. Additionally, doors and windows should have screens (mosquito netting) that allow air to pass through while keeping out flying insects and creepy crawlers. Also, the doors and windows must have flaps that allow them to be closed for privacy and to keep out the rain thrown horizontally by driving winds.
3. *You need a tent you can pitch (set up) with ease.* You want to pitch your tent easily and quickly (see Chapter 4), especially when you arrive after dark or

you're hurrying to get it done before heavy clouds start to spill their accumulated wetness. Tents you can pitch easily are also easier to strike (take down), a plus when you're running late.

4. *You need a tent with enough room inside.* Tent manufacturers tend to rate size by suggesting how many people will fit inside. They'll say, for example, this is a "two-person tent" or that is a "four-person tent." Remember, they are making *suggestions.* You must step into, lie down in, and move around inside a tent to be sure it has enough room for you. Two people, of course, will be more comfortable in a much smaller tent than will a family of five. Even so, some campers prefer a tent with lots of headroom to allow standing, while some are satisfied with only crawl space. When you think about size, think about this: what if it rains all day? You need enough room not only for sleeping but also for everyone to stretch out with a book or to gather around a board game. Since weight won't matter—the vehicle, remember, is right there—choose a tent with ample space inside.

5. *You'll enjoy a tent that comes with "extras."* Generally speaking, the more extras a tent has, the more it will cost. However, those extras—such as storage pockets sewn to the insides of the walls, nylon loops inside for hanging this and that, interior clotheslines, and two-way zippers on doors and windows—can add a lot to camping ease and comfort. Another extra feature worth considering is a vestibule, a small extension from the main body of a tent within which you can handily store gear.

TIP

THE COLOR OF A TENT: You're likely to have a choice of color when you select your tent. You'll probably appreciate a lighter color, such as yellow, tan, white, or pale blue, because it will let in more natural light.

TECHNO: TENTS

POLES: At setup time, the job is easiest when you either (a) slip the tent poles into sleeves that are an integral part of the tent or (b) attach the tent to the poles with clips. Spend a few extra dollars on shock-corded poles—the shock cords are elastic bands inside the poles that connect all the parts of a pole as a unit. Because they stay together when they're packed and when they're being used to

Continued

pitch the tent, they shave a lot of frustration, as well as minutes, off pitching and striking time. The poles will be made of one of the following materials:

Aluminum—strong, fairly light, not too expensive, a good choice.

Fiberglass—breaks more easily than aluminum unless made with carbon fiber, which costs more.

Stainless steel—heavier, very strong, unnecessary except for very heavy tents.

STAKES: Your tent will come with stakes, but they might not work well in every environment where you set your tent. Slim metal stakes, for example, work well in firm soil such as you find in a forest, but they pull out too easily in sandy soil. In loose, sandy soil or beach sand, you want longer, wider plastic stakes.

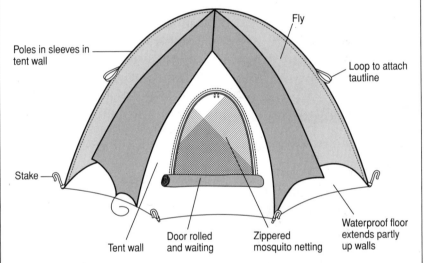

Poles in sleeves in tent wall

Fly

Loop to attach tautline

Stake

Tent wall

Door rolled and waiting

Zippered mosquito netting

Waterproof floor extends partly up walls

The anatomy of a tent

SEASONS: *Four-season tents* are made of extra-tough nylon and usually come with at least four poles. They are made to withstand the winter stresses of snow loads and hard winds. You're almost always well advised to avoid the extra expense of a four-season tent.

Three-season tents are made to stand up to the vagaries of weather from spring through fall. Unless you plan on an early spring or late fall camping trip, you won't need to pay the cost of a three-season tent—but, then again, you may enjoy the security of having one.

Summer/two-season tents are designed to ward off the occasional shower and relatively stiff winds, but little more. Summer tents, on the plus side, often have a lot of mosquito netting, allowing excellent ventilation and less of an enclosed feeling. Most campers do well with a summer tent.

Tent Shapes

Quite a few tents out there have very odd shapes. Some claim to be oddly shaped for a reason, and some seem to be odd for the sake of oddness. But if you stand back far enough, you'll see there are really only four basic shapes to choose from—each with advantages and disadvantages.

Dome Tents

A *dome* is the most popular shape today. You'll see them squared off, rectangular, even geodesic in design, but they all look sort of like colorful igloos. All are typically very easy to pitch. The rounded, arching walls allow you to use pretty much all the floor space while providing adequate headroom. They are free-standing, which means you don't need stakes and taut lines to hold them up. You can easily

Dome tents are sort of like colorful igloos.

pick up and move a free-standing tent. You will, however, want to use stakes once you set the tent where you want it, to keep it from moving around. Staked out, domes shed wind and water, from all directions, better than any other shape. Unstaked, they make great kites without strings in very little wind.

A-frame Tents

The basic *A-frame* shape has been around for centuries. Tie a line between two trees, throw a piece of canvas over it, stake down the corners, and you have an A-frame. Modern A-frames are much nicer, and some are free-standing. The steeply sloped walls shed water well, but wind usually keeps the nylon flapping noisily. The steep slope of A-frame walls makes virtually useless much of the floor space where the steep walls meet the floor.

A-frame tents are the simplest design.

Wall Tents

Wall (or cabin) tents are most like a room at home.

A *wall tent*, sometimes called a cabin tent, stands more like a room of a house than any other tent shape. The tent walls are vertical, and the roof slopes enough to shed water. You'll find more useable space inside than in any other shape. Some wall tents even have multiple rooms and/or a screened section, sort of like a screened patio. These are, as you can imagine, the most difficult to pitch, and they're the most difficult to manage in wind. You may also find a hard rain difficult to keep out. Wall tents are typically not free-standing.

Partial-dome Tents

A *partial-dome* tent combines some of the features of a wall tent with some of

A partial-dome tent combines features of a dome tent and a wall tent.

the features of a dome. The walls are gently sloped, providing plenty of floor space and shedding wind better than vertical walls, and the relatively high ceiling gives you lots of headroom. The tent itself is usually free-standing, but the fly, which gives it the partial dome shape, must typically be staked out. These pitch more easily than a wall tent but with more difficulty than a dome or an A-frame. Partial-dome tents sometimes have a built-in front awning, which provides a useful covered area.

Tarps

Although you can, you'll seldom choose to sleep under a tarp. There's no mosquito netting, no floor, no storage pockets, nothing to stop a hard wind from curling underneath. But many campers always pack a tarp. On a rainy day, a tarp can be

A tarp can serve many useful functions.

set up over the cooking area, set up as a large extension of the tent, or set up over the tent for additional protection. On sunny days, a tarp provides shade.

A sheet of inexpensive plastic can serve as a tarp. Tie a line between two trees, throw the plastic over it, and tie off the corners with cord. Be sure to fold a small rock into each corner of the plastic first, providing a point around which to tie the cord. A *real* tarp, with grommets set at regular intervals along the edge, is much easier to tie down.

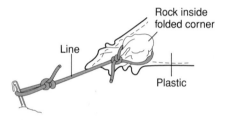

Line

Rock inside folded corner

Plastic

Tying the corners of a sheet of plastic to make an improvised tarp.

TIP

TARP GAMES: In a heavy downpour, you can set up a tarp as an extension of your van or camper. With the vehicle's rear access open, let the kids play inside while you sit on a camp chair and cook dinner on a stove under the tarp. It doesn't have to be a huge tarp—10 feet by 10 feet will seldom fail to be large enough.

TECHNO: SEALING SEAMS

With tent or tarp, the seams must be sealed to keep out water. Some seams are factory sealed. If they aren't, you must apply to the seams, at least once every season, a seam-sealing product. Before sealing the seams, set up the tent and let it stand for an hour or so. The holes where the seams are stitched will stretch a bit, and thus you'll be able to fill them completely when you apply the seam sealer. Allow the seam-sealing product to dry completely before storing the tent.

The Bedroom

The tent will serve primarily, as mentioned previously, as the bedroom. Without sound sleep you probably won't have a great camping experience—and that means you need not only a good space to sleep in (the tent) but also a good bed to sleep in.

Sleeping Pads

Starting from the tent floor, a good bed requires a good mattress (a sleeping pad). You can cover yourself adequately with almost anything (see "Padding for the Night") and still sleep poorly on a bad mattress. Pads soften the hard ground—a mighty big plus—and they also prevent the loss of body heat into cold ground. Outdoor mattress technology has benefited from remarkable innovations in recent years.

Mama Kristin Speaks

If the kids are five or older, consider housing your family in two separate, smaller tents. More fun for them, more fun for you! Plus, should any of you delve into the world of backpacking someday, you won't need to buy a new shelter, since you'll already own a smaller, more lightweight tent suitable for backpacking.

TECHNO: PADDING FOR THE NIGHT

The basic choices in sleeping pads are these:

Air Mattresses. Although they've been around a long time, *air mattresses* have improved in recent years. They're lighter and stronger. A bit of huffing and puffing, provided by your lungs, is still required to inflate these pads to fatness—unless you pack a pump with which to blow them up. Air mattresses come in two basic styles: one that holds the air in tubes that run the length of the mattress, and one that holds the air in a single, large chamber. Experiment to see which one feels better to you. Either style can rupture, leaving you flat. High-quality air mattresses are relatively expensive, but some brands don't cost much at all.

Self-Inflating Mattresses. Most recent innovations have been in *self-inflating mattresses,* such as Therm-a-Rest pads. You open a valve and relax while the air rushes in. A couple of your added breaths will firm one up, and the result is excellent comfort. Though they are available in different widths and lengths and thicknesses you'll get maximum comfort from a wide, long,

A good night's sleep starts with a good pad, such as this Therm-a-Rest.

Continued

thick pad—which costs a bit more. If you choose one with a nonslip surface, you will not find yourself half on the ground in the morning—or worse, during a cold night. On the downside, they can spring a leak, but the best ones come with a repair kit. It's worthwhile getting a repair kit if the manufacturer doesn't provide one since duct tape won't suffice if your mattress springs a leak. Covers are available that add additional protection for the pad and fold into a chair for camp lounging.

Closed-Cell Foam Pads. Virtually indestructible, *closed-cell foam pads* are lightweight and relatively comfortable—but far from the comfort of a self-inflating mattress. As with self-inflating pads, they will not absorb moisture, and they cost much less than self-inflating pads. The foam is dense and semi-rigid, and the pads do a fair job of insulating you from cold ground.

Open-Cell Foam Pads. Least expensive and least comfortable, *open-cell foam pads* are much less dense than closed cell. They are spongy to the touch, allowing that twig you didn't remove from under the tent to jab you all night, and they soak up water like a sponge. If you choose an open-cell foam pad, try to find one with a waterproof cover.

TIPS

DECADENT SLEEPING PAD WISDOM: It's totally okay to use two sleeping pads. You'll have a thicker bed (cushy) and more insulation from the ground (warmer).

FLAT-FREE SLEEPING: You can reduce the chance of a leak by not over-inflating an air mattress. You don't have to blow in all the air you can—only enough for a comfy sleep.

Cots

Most campers lay their mattresses on their tent floors, but some tents are large enough to allow use of camp cots. If you use a cot, you'll still need a mattress for a sound sleep. Some cots have end bars at head and foot, which is a problem if you're longer than the cot. The point is, once again, to try it before you buy it. Also note the legs of the cot. Tubular legs are rounded and easy on tent floors while straight legs torture tent floors.

A cot with tubular legs and an air mattress on top

Sleeping Bags

As with tents, sleeping bags must meet your demands. Summer-only campers may do well with comforters or blankets, though if you don't own sleeping bags, you probably will eventually. Sleeping bags are the most practical form of bedding for camping. They stuff into a fairly small sack, yet they keep you warmer than blankets if you camp when the temperature dips into the chilly to downright cold range.

With literally hundreds of sleeping bags to choose from, picking one might at first seem an insurmountable challenge. It is a challenge, but it's certainly not insurmountable. Reduced to the basics, a bag must keep you warm and dry, and—if you've chosen well—comfortable. It's a matter of the materials used, and the way the materials are put together.

SLEEPING BAG KNOW-HOW:

TIP

1. Your sleeping bag came with a stuff sack. It's called a "stuff sack" because you should grab handfuls of the bag and stuff it in. Don't try to roll the bag first. Stuffing is easier on you, and actually easier on the fabric and the insulation of the bag.
2. Unstuff your bag with gentle, steady tugs. Yanking a bag out of its sack can damage the material of the bag.
3. Keep your bag off the ground to keep it clean and extend its life. Stuff it and unstuff it inside the tent or onto a ground cloth.
4. When not in use, store your bag loose (see Chapter 11).

Sleeping Warm

Sleeping bags will have a *temperature rating*. This tells you how cold it can be outside your bag while you remain warm inside. The lower the temperature rating, the warmer you will be in the bag, and as the rating goes down the price goes up in almost all cases. Unfortunately, the rating acts as a guide only. No absolute standard exists, and you might feel cold—and cheated—in a bag rated to keep you warm. Unfortunately, you'll have to sleep in a specific bag to know for sure how it will suit you, but the following chart will give you a rough guideline.

Ratings Chart

Bag Temperature Rating	Season
32 degrees F or higher	Summer
20–32 degrees F	Late spring to early fall
0–20 degrees F	Early spring to late fall
0 degrees F or lower	Winter

If you're going to be doing most of your camping in the balmy summer months, you'll want to be careful not to select a bag that is rated to keep you too warm.

Insulation

Sleeping bags are stuffed with *insulation* to hold in your body heat. The insulation fluffs up and traps dead air around your body. Your body heat warms the dead air, and the air stays warm through the night—so you sleep warm. The insulation in bags will be either a synthetic material or down (the small inner feathers of certain birds), and both may be referred to as the "fill."

Synthetic fills are made from plastic fibers, and they have a variety of interesting names: Polarguard, Hollofil, Quallofil, Primaloft, Thinsulate, and so on. They all have specific differences, but they're all much less expensive than down, require less care, and dry much faster if they get wet. On the negative side—but not too negative—synthetics are heavier than down, and, for the weight, they don't keep you as warm as down. Since weight won't be a problem for the type of camping you'll be doing, synthetic bags are almost always the best bet.

If you want a *down* bag, you'll have choices of how much down and what kind of down have been used to fill a bag. The larger the number of the down fill, the more down you'll have as insulation. A 750 down fill, for example, gives you more insulation than a 550 down fill. The more down fill, as you can imagine, the more you'll have to pay for the bag. Prime goose down makes the best insulation—and the most expensive. You'll also find very fine bags with less-than-prime goose down and duck down.

TECHNO: SLEEPING BAG CONSTRUCTION

If the insulation is sewn into pockets, or cells, in your sleeping bag to keep it from shifting around, cold can creep in through the seams between the pockets. Well-made bags are baffled with interior walls that overlap to prevent exposed seams, but baffled bags cost more. If you don't plan to camp in the cold, you won't usually need baffling—but if you can afford a bag with baffling, you may appreciate it on a surprisingly cold night.

AN OLD BLANKET: Throw an old blanket in the vehicle. If your sleeping pad isn't thick enough, fold the blanket and put it under your pad for extra protection. If you get chilled from exposed seams or cool air slipping in around the zipper, add the blanket over your sleeping bag.

Sleeping Dry

Sure, rain may fly in through an open tent window or water may creep in through a poorly constructed tent floor, but most of the moisture that dampens a sleeping bag comes from your body. Sleeping bags are constructed with an outer *shell* and an inner *lining,* and the best shells and liners "breathe" to allow your body moisture to escape. Bags that don't breathe can become a mini-sauna on a warm night.

DEFINING TERMS

A *draft tube* is a layer of insulation sewn into a tube that overlaps a zipper when it's closed. Without a draft tube, a zipper can become a bothersome escape route for your body heat. It doesn't take much chill for the unbaffled zipper on your sleeping bag to keep you awake.

A *one-way zipper* zips up and down only one way. A *two-way zipper* opens and closes from the top or the bottom. Two-way zippers cost more, but in a sleeping bag they're a nice extra, allowing you to ventilate the bottom of the bag on a too-warm night while keeping your shoulders covered.

TECHNO: SLEEPING BAG SHAPES

Mummy bags are narrow at the feet, wider at the shoulders, and have a hood that can be closed around your head. You end up in a cocoon, and body heat retention is maximized—but, because of their shape, these bags provide less sleeping room. Mummies also tend to be the most expensive bags.

King Tut would fit nicely in this mummy bag.

Rectangular bags are squared at the four corners, and they provide plenty of tossing and turning room. Since they stay open at your head, they simply aren't as warm to sleep in as mummies. They are heavier than mummies, take up more room in a pack, and therefore are seldom chosen by backpackers. Rectangular bags are, however, often chosen by tent campers, especially those who primarily camp in summer, and they are usually the least expensive.

Continued

A rectangular bag made especially with kids in mind

Semi-rectangular bags have some characteristics of mummy and rectangular bags. Some will close around your head the way a mummy bag does, and some won't. Semi-rectangular bags may be the best choice when your camping trips start early in the year and extend into fall.

SLEEPING BAG SIZES: Sleeping bags vary in length and width. To better meet sleeping needs, some bag manufacturers offer lengths and widths designed especially for women and children. The point is this: before buying a bag, get in and zip it up and roll around. Choose a bag that fits. Extra room means extra air space your body has to heat, but extra room usually means a more comfortable sleep.

TIP

PAJAMA PARTY: Wearing an extra layer or two of clothing in a tight-fitting bag compresses and, therefore, reduces the value of the insulation. However, if you get chilled in a roomy bag, you can sleep in comfortable clothing, such as long underwear, to up your chances of a restful night. A roomy tent/car camping bag is a fine idea.

TECHNO: ZIP-TOGETHER SLEEPING BAGS

Some sleeping bags may be purchased in pairs that zip together. You end up with a space greater than the sum of the parts. In other words, you have lots more room in zip-together bags. Some couples prefer to sleep in zip-together bags with a wee one between them. Some couples prefer zip-together bags for other understandable reasons.

TIP

PILLOW TALK: You'll sleep better with a pillow. You can roll clothing into a serviceable pillow, but why not pack a pillow for everybody? You can purchase camp pillows, or you can take them from home. If you're worried about ruining a good pillow in camp—and you might—pack only pillowcases and stuff them with extra clothing until you've created a pillow of just the right dimensions.

The Kitchen

Nowhere do you find more variety in camps than in the kitchen. On the quick-and-easy end of things, you'll see appetites apparently satisfied by cheese and crackers washed down with a can of soda and topped off with a candy bar. If that sort of menu works for you, your camp kitchen will be extremely simple—and your camping experience will be greatly diminished. Consider, on the other end of things, steaks sizzling on a grill while biscuits bake in a Dutch oven, spicy beans simmer in a pot, and the smell of hot coffee wafts through the trees. There will be times when you want something fast, yes, and other times when life is all about dinner. Deciding what you want to eat will determine what you need to pack for your kitchen—and in the following subsections are some guidelines.

Stoves

Anything that can be cooked can be cooked on a fire (see Chapter 7), but stoves are easier and faster. You should pack a stove even if you plan to cook on fires. There may be fire restrictions, a lack of firewood, or torrents of rain. Which stove to choose? Once again, the answer is this: it depends.

This two-burner stove runs off a propane cartridge.

Large Stoves

In most cases, you'll appreciate packing a large camp stove, one with at least two burners. Who wants to start the day with coffee that cooled off while the pancakes fried—or vice versa. If you have a large family, plan to entertain guests, or just enjoy more involved meals, consider a three-burner. Choose one that closes up neatly for packing.

- You can purchase a large stove with folding legs and foldout wings. It's a stove built into a meal-prep table.
- You can purchase a folding "kitchen"—storage space, counter space, and stove space built into one unit.

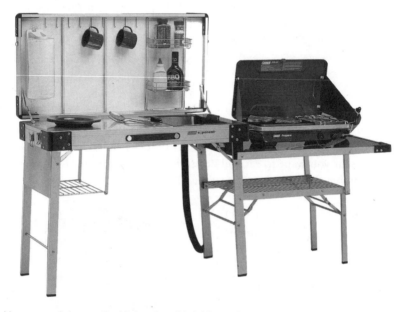

You can pack your entire kitchen into this folding unit.

Types of Large Stoves

The type of stove is determined by the type of fuel it uses.

Liquid-fuel stoves run on either white gas or unleaded fuel. Some will operate on white gas *and* unleaded fuel, both of which you'll carry in separate fuel containers from which you'll fill the fuel tank of the stove. You'll have to pump up the pressure on the stove's tank before the fuel will be delivered to the burners. With the fuel pressurized, you'll ignite it with a match or, if you've spent a bit more money, with the stove's electric ignition. Over a long cooking time, the pressure may weaken, requiring renewed pumping. Liquid fuel is inexpensive, and a gallon will last a long time. On the downside, there's lot to fiddle with—the pouring, the pumping, and the storing and handling of a highly flammable liquid.

Propane stoves are fueled in one of two ways: (a) from a single-use cartridge of propane that screws onto the stove or (b) from a separate, and much larger, refillable propane tank that attaches to the stove via a hose. Use is safe and easy. All you do is attach the source of propane, turn a knob, and light a burner. The flame from propane is more consistent than that from liquid fuel. On the downside, propane and propane stoves cost more, and you often can't find more propane if you run out while away from home.

A small one-burner stove may meet your needs.

Small Stoves

A small, lightweight, one-burner camp stove may be great for simple one-pot meals or just boiling water. Backpackers pull out these stoves after a long day on the trail. There are many to choose from, and they vary widely in cost. You can find small, one-burners that operate off a disposable butane or propane cartridge.

Types of Small Stoves

Once again, the "type" of stove is determined by the fuel.

Kerosene is cheap, but it stinks, burns without producing as much heat as other fuels, and tends to coat everything with a greasy film. Kerosene does not deserve much consideration.

Butane and propane come in cartridges that pack neatly, light quickly without priming, and burn cleanly. They do not burn as hot as white gas, but they do the job. One instance when they might fail you is when the temperature is low. Cartridges tend to put out too little effort on a cold day. The gas can freeze in the cartridge on a really cold day, but you can keep it warm by keeping it in your sleeping bag while you sleep. However, sleeping with it does not solve another problem: almost all cartridges do not let you see how much fuel is left. Without another cartridge on hand, you may find yourself with a half-cooked meal.

White gas is carried in a separate container from which you fill the stove every day. It burns very hot and clean no matter how low the temperature sinks and is virtually odorless. Does white gas have problems? Yes. For one thing it requires priming. A well-made small stove comes with a built-in priming mechanism that almost always works. Squeeze tubes of primer can be purchased for emergencies. If a hot stove blows out in a stiff wind, it is often difficult to restart until it has cooled. White-gas stoves must be pumped to place the fuel under enough pressure to rise to the burner. Though liquid fuel is extremely flammable, white gas generally works best to fuel a small stove, all things considered.

Cookware

Here's an area of the kitchen, and the camp, where you can get by just fine with items you use at home. You don't need, in other words, to go shopping for cookware—just grab some pots and pans from the kitchen cabinet. But don't grab your best. Camp life can be hard on cookware. There's always a chance, of course, that you'll become an avid camper and that you'll want to have a set of camping cookware—including utensils, cups, plates, and such—stored together and ready to load quickly when a weekend outdoors is just too appealing to stay at home.

TECHNO: WHAT'S A POT MADE OF?

Aluminum: The lightest and cheapest material used to make pots and pans—and the best choice for most campers. If the pot has an interior nonstick coating, you'll reduce the chance of scorching and speed up cleaning.

Stainless steel: More durable than aluminum, and more expensive, but a good choice if you want your camp cookware to last a long time.

Cast-iron: If you want your camp cookware to last longer than you, go with cast iron, which is excellent for cooking but takes more care than aluminum and stainless steel—for example, it can rust (see Chapter 7).

Pots and Pans

The size and number of pots and pans you carry must correspond to the number of campers in your group and to the complexity of your meals. If, for example, you only plan to boil water for two, one small pot will do. If you're planning spaghetti with meat sauce, boiled corn, and hot tea for six, you'd better have three large pots and a frying pan. Often listed in liters, a 1-liter pot will hold slightly less than a quart. Pans are typically listed in inches describing their diameter. Here's a guide:

- A *1-liter pot* (approximately 1 quart) will boil a few cups of water for hot chocolate or two small servings of pasta. It also can serve as a saucepan for more involved meals.
- A *1.5-liter pot* (approximately 1.5 quarts) is large enough to cook one-pot meals for an average couple or for side dishes in a bigger party.
- A *2-liter pot* (approximately 2 quarts) has room for enough water to make hot chocolate for six or one dinner entrée for three hungry campers.
- A *3-liter pot* (approximately 3 quarts) gives you enough capacity to cook up an entrée for six or more campers.
- A *10- to 12-inch-diameter frying pan* will do in most camps. A smaller one will often work for a couple. If your pan has a snug-fitting lid, carry it. A pan with a lid can be used for baking (see Chapter 7).

Lightweight camping cookware with potgrips

TIP

SHOPPING FOR THE KITCHEN: You can find all you need at outdoor specialty stores and websites, such as GSI Outdoors, from low-tech (a plastic cup) to incredibly high-tech (a camp blender). At garage sales and the big discount houses, you also can find great items that will provide excellent service.

TECHNO: COOKWARE

- Choose camp cookware that comes with snug-fitting lids: water will boil faster, thus saving fuel and time. A lid also keeps out smoke and ash if you try your hand at campfire cooking (see Chapter 7). If you don't have a lid, a frying pan often can substitute as a lid.
- Choose camp cookware that comes with handles. Some camp cookware pots have a bail handle, like the handle on a bucket. These wire loops let you grab and carry big pots with ease. Caution is required, though, because these handles get hot when they're attached to a pot you're heating. Some pots have swing handles that are attached to the cookware, and they swing out from the side of a pot or flip out from inside a frying pan.
- Some camp cookware pots have lipped rims that curve gently to the outside to make a pot easier to grab with potgrips and less prone to bending and warping under the pressure of gripping with potgrips.
- Modern camp cookware often comes with a dark exterior finish. The dark color maximizes the speed at which pots heat, and it holds the heat longer.
- Modern camp cookware often comes with rounded bottom edges. This feature encourages even heat distribution up the walls of the pot and eliminates hard-to-clean messes in the corners.

CAMP KITCHEN ORGANIZATION: Pots, pans, cups, bowls, spoons, knives, spices, paper towels, soap! There's a heap of stuff to pack for a camp kitchen. One of those large plastic bins available for very little money at discount stores will serve well to keep it all together. Or you may choose a higher level of sophistication and organize your entire kitchen in a utility box designed especially for that purpose. Homemade models, some of them very nice, all of them very heavy, occasionally appear in a neighboring campsite. Go for it if you're handy with a saw and a hammer, but you may decide to purchase a camp kitchen utility box with several thousand cubic inches of storage, including space for a large stove, plenty of pots and pans, spices, a silverware tray, and more.

Additional Camping Cookware

- *Coffeepot.* You can always throw instant coffee into a cup of hot water, or a handful of ground coffee into a pot of hot water, but a coffeepot should be considered by those who enjoy a finely brewed cup or two.
- *Dutch oven.* A cast-iron Dutch oven is like a frying pan with high sides (the kettle), and the better ones have three short legs. It should come with a snug-fitting lid, and the lid should have a raised rim for holding hot coals. Good ones come with a strong handle, or bail, for easy lifting and moving. A Dutch oven

A Dutch oven is the most versatile piece of camping cookware.

is, simply put, the most versatile piece of camp cookware. Adaptable to any kind of cooking—boiling, baking, frying, stewing, poaching—they can sit on your stove, stand on a grate over a fire, or be nestled directly in the hot coals of a fire. You can flip the lid over and use it as a griddle. Dutch oven cooking, which is rapidly becoming a lost art, is worthy of your consideration (see Chapter 7). You'll find these sized from 8 inches in diameter for two people to 22-inch

DEFINING TERMS

Potgrips are tools somewhat like a pair of pliers designed specifically to grab and lift a hot pot. You also can use pliers or a multi-use tool as potgrips.

monsters that can produce enough grub for a soccer team. A family, small to medium in size, will do well with a 12-inch Dutch oven.

- *Griddle.* A griddle that fits over two or three burners on your stove will allow you to fry bacon and eggs or flip some flapjacks for a large number of people at the same time.
- *Camping Oven.* If you like to bake, or you can talk someone into doing the baking, camping ovens are made for the job. The Outback Oven, for example, sits over a burner of your stove; heat is circulated around this pan by a convection dome, and you can whip up any baked goods from bread to brownies.

TABLECLOTH: Picnic tabletops at campgrounds tend to be unappealingly messy. Some of the debris can be brushed off—leaves, pine needles—but some of it may be ground in—dirt, bird droppings, the remains of the last camper's dinner. For that reason, carrying an inexpensive, plastic tablecloth is a fine idea.

Utensils

You'll want a spoon, fork, knife, plate, and maybe a bowl for just about everyone in camp. Paper and plastic will work fine in most cases. If you purchase camping utensils, consider Lexan, a light, strong, and durable plastic that doesn't cost very much. Alternatively, you can make a pass through your home kitchen. You'll want a cup for everyone in your group. Inexpensive insulated mugs with snug-fitting lids keep hot drinks hot, cold drinks cold, and insects and debris out of your beverage of choice, and they are available at convenience stores everywhere.

Sets of camping utensils are available with almost everything you need.

TIPS

IMPROVISING IN THE KITCHEN: You can recycle margarine or yogurt tubs for bowls and cups, or you can use Tupperware containers from home.

DID YOU BRING THE . . . ?:

- *Spatula:* You may want one to flip the hamburger patties.
- *Large knife:* To slice veggies or anything else.
- *Cutting board:* Not necessary— but nice.
- *Ladle:* For serving hot soup and beverages.
- *Can opener:* If you're carrying canned food.
- *Measuring cup:* Or you can make your best guess.
- *Corkscrew:* Or you'll have to dig out the cork in your wine bottle.

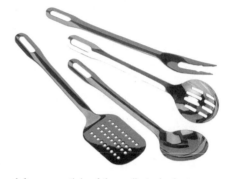

A few essentials of the well-stocked camp kitchen

KEEPING UTENSILS HANDY:

- Purchase a *kitchen kit:* a handy zippered bag that comes filled with the basic camping utensils.
- Use a *multipocket carpenter's apron* to hold your cooking utensils. Tie it around a tree trunk at eye level near your cooking area.

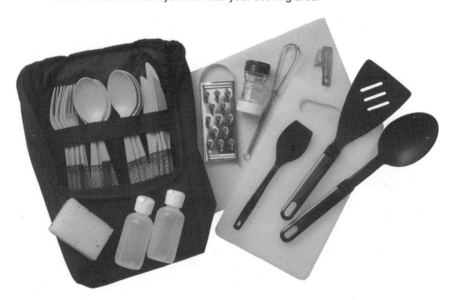

Kitchen kits are available with all the basics in a handy zippered bag.

Camp Kitchen Cleanup

You'll need some dish soap, and low-phosphate/biodegradable products are a bit easier on the environment. You'll want a scrubbing sponge for those food scraps that cling tenaciously to your pots. You can do a more-than-adequate job of washing the dishes (and the rest of your camp kitchen gear) in a sturdy, inexpensive plastic tub. Warm water in a pot over the fire or on the stove, and you're ready to clean. With a second tub, you can rinse in cold water after adding just enough bleach to give the water a faint chlorine odor. Or you can fill a second tub with warm water for rinsing. Wipe off the rinsed gear with a clean towel—and store everything for the night.

DECADENT DISH WASHING: If you're inclined toward more convenience, portable hot water heaters are available. The Coleman Company, for example, offers a hot-water-on-demand heater that turns cold water into 100-degree water in about five seconds. Be prepared for a substantial price tag: these heaters cost in the neighborhood of $200.

TIP

Food

The advice here, generally speaking, is pretty simple: take what you like to eat. You might be surprised, however, how far toward culinary excellence your camp meals can reach: hot biscuits, delicious one-pot stews, fresh-baked brownies. (If you want to try some tried-and-true recipes when you camp, see Chapter 7.) If you can imagine it, you can whip it up in an outdoor kitchen. Culinary excellence aside, the following are some thoughts on camp food:

1. Don't forget the refrigerator, in this case a *cooler.* Some are simply insulated boxes. Soft coolers are made from an insulating fabric. The hard box-type cooler prevents food items from being crushed. Some have a tray to store foods you don't want directly in contact with the ice or with melting ice, such as lettuce and sandwiches. You can even find expensive coolers with a built-in, battery-powered light for nighttime rummaging in the "fridge."

2. Drinks can be kept cold in large, insulated jugs with easy-pour spouts. You'll save a lot of cooler space that way.

3. If you don't want to cook in camp, prepare meals at home and store them in

boiling-safe plastic bags. In camp, set the bag in boiling water until it heats up. If you freeze the meals ahead of time, you can use them as ice in your cooler.

4. Buy foods such as mustard, mayonnaise, jam, and peanut butter in squeeze-type containers. These containers prevent dirt and debris from getting into open jars, and they make serving easier.

5. Canned foods don't usually taste the best, but they are easy to transport, store, and prepare at mealtime.

6. Don't forget a spice kit. Salt and pepper, and a few of your favorite spices, can add much to mealtime.

COOLER TIPS:

TIP

1. If you don't have a storage tray in your cooler, put foods you don't want to get wet in zip-top plastic bags.

2. Whatever cooler you choose, use block ice. Block ice lasts much longer than crushed ice.

3. To extend the life of your ice keep the cooler open no longer than necessary.

4. Pre-cool in your refrigerator at home the food you'll carry in your cooler.

5. Wrap the cooler in a blanket for more insulation during travel time in your vehicle, and keep the cooler in a shady spot in camp.

6. The next time you buy ice cream at the market, you might be offered an insulated bag to keep the ice cream colder on the way home. Save the insulated bag, and use it for frozen food you carry in your cooler.

7. If you don't like the mess of melting ice—and it will eventually melt— purchase reusable plastic freezer packs, the ones you freeze at home and use again and again in your cooler.

Water

You'll need water, and most campgrounds will have a source—but it might be quite a walk from your campsite to the faucet. Carry a large rigid or collapsible water container, one that holds three to five gallons. You may also bring water from home in a large container to save time at camp. In all cases, you'll be happier if the container has a spout with a spigot. Set the container on the edge of a picnic table so you can fill a cup or pot with ease.

Mama Kristin Speaks

Before your trip, raid your recycle bin for used plastic water bottles. Wash and fill almost to the top (liquid expands when it freezes) with your kids' favorite juice. Freeze the bottles overnight, then pack them in your cooler. The frozen bottles will help chill your food, and once thawed your kids can guzzle the cold juice.

PURCHASE WATER: If you don't have a water container, stop by a market and pick up a couple of large containers of water with turn-handle spouts.

TIP

The Bathroom

The campground will almost always provide some sort of rest room. On one end of the spectrum of possibilities, it might be a simple pit toilet—a modern version of the ubiquitous outhouse of yore. Toward the other end, you'll find well-lit buildings with flush toilets and sinks with cold and hot running water. You might even find a full-service bathhouse with hot showers and, now and then, a laundry room. When a rest room is provided, use it. You may have enough privacy to urinate behind a tree, but the campground will benefit if you don't. If you find none of these amenities, you'll have to create bathroom "facilities" for yourself (see Chapter 10).

BATHROOM TIPS:

TIP

1. Always carry a roll of toilet paper—or two, or more. The dispenser in the rest room might be empty when you most need it.
2. Pack separate towels for everybody. You may not be able to take a shower, but you'll be able to dry off thoroughly after washing your hands or other body parts. You also may want to dry off after a walk in the rain, after a swim, or after accidentally flipping your canoe, your kayak, or such.
3. Consider, also, carrying a large, inexpensive plastic tub. If the campground has no sinks, a tub of warm water will make washing your face and hands much more pleasant—and you'll have much more thorough results. If you brought a tub to use in the camp kitchen, you can, of course, use the same tub for personal washing.

The Clothes Closet

This section covers clothing from head to toe. For the tent camper, choosing what clothing to take along can involve no more than a trip to your closet and digging

- Undergarments
- Mid-layer garments (shirts, sweaters, jackets, vests, pants)
- Outer-layer garments, often called "shells" and including rainwear and parkas
- Accessory clothing, such as hats, gloves, and bandannas
- Footwear

through a couple of drawers. Anything looking kind of worn will suffice—as long as you don't care if it gets more worn. The wise camper, however, *understands* clothing. Outdoor clothing choices increase in importance depending on what activities you plan to do. If, say, you intend to hike far away from your campsite, you need clothing that protects you from changes in the weather. What you wear either adds to or subtracts from what your body is trying to do on its own: maintain a normal core temperature (see "Categories of Camping Clothes"). Jeans and a cotton sweatshirt might serve you well in camp but not if a sudden shower soaks you away from camp.

Understanding Clothing Materials

A lot of what clothing does for you depends on the material used to make it.

Cotton

Almost everyone agrees that cotton is the most comfortable fabric to wear against skin. Because cotton "breathes" well, it allows perspiration to escape into the air easily, and that's good on a warm day. Cotton also absorbs lots of water, and that increases the rate at which you lose heat on a cold day. You have probably stood outside sometime in a wet tee shirt and felt the heat rushing out of your body. Thus, cotton is an excellent choice on summer days in hot regions. Cotton's tendency to cool you rapidly makes it an extremely poor, and often dangerous, choice for colder environments. In summary, cotton works efficiently as a thermal conductor, which means it does *not* work well as insulation against cold.

Wool

Wool has been worn for centuries by people around the world who spend time outdoors. It offers a lot of advantages over cotton. Wool fibers, being heavier and coarser than cotton, conduct heat poorly, which means they provide excellent insulation. Wool keeps much of its ability to insulate even when wet. Unprocessed ("virgin") wool retains oil from the sheep that it once covered, allowing it to dry much faster than cotton. You can wring water from wool clothing, put it on again, and wear it all day without losing much body heat. And if the rain stops, wool will dry, although very slowly, while you wear it. Wool is also more durable than cotton.

Wool does have its downside. It tends to be heavy and bulky compared to cotton, especially when wet, and it takes more care. Most wool, for example, shrinks when washed in hot water or left in the clothes dryer. Some people cannot stand the feel of wool against their skin. Those people will be happy to know that some new wool clothing has been manufactured in a way that makes it quite soft against your skin. These newer wool garments, however, cost more.

Synthetics

Synthetics are petroleum products, and they are used to make socks and caps and everything in between that covers your body. In simple terms, synthetics are made from plastic woven into thread that is woven into clothing. When used for clothing, synthetics may be referred to as "pile" or "fleece." Synthetic fibers are stuffed into synthetic shells to make parkas for extremes of cold. Synthetics conduct little heat, even less than wool, making them the best choice for staying warm. Synthetics absorb almost no water, and they actually transport moisture away from your skin, a process referred to as "wicking," which makes them the best choice for staying dry. They are lighter than wool and stand up fairly well to hard use. An added bonus: some manufacturers create their fleece from recycled materials such as plastic pop bottles, keeping them out of landfills.

In the minus column, synthetics, being plastic, melt at relatively low temperatures. You can ruin a good pair of synthetic gloves just by picking up a hot pot. Unless you purchase special wind-blocking fleece, synthetics allow icy breezes to blow through freely. Also, synthetics tend to hold onto bad odors such as those produced by a sweaty body.

Just the Facts: How You Maintain Body Heat

Your body must balance the heat it makes from the food you eat with the heat you lose to the environment. You lose heat in four ways:

- *Conduction.* When you touch cold surfaces, heat is drawn out of your body. Adequate clothing prevents conductive heat loss.
- *Convection.* Wind slicing through your clothing tears away a thin layer of heat that your body immediately replaces. In a high wind you can lose a substantial amount of heat in a short period of time. You need clothing that will keep out wind.
- *Radiation.* Exposed skin radiates a significant amount of heat into the surrounding environment. Clothing slows or stops radiative heat loss.
- *Evaporation.* Heat escapes your body through the vaporization of moisture, which is the major source of body heat loss. On a cold day, the evaporation of sweat or water from your skin can suck a tremendous amount of heat out of your body. Clothing must allow sweat to exit without vaporizing and taking body heat with it.

Clothes for Warm Weather

Shorts
tee shirts
Lightweight trousers
Lightweight, long-sleeved shirt
Wide-brimmed hat
Raingear
Bandanna
Light fleece layer, including a cap
(to be safe)

Warm Weather Clothing

Naturally, you are not going to worry as much about maintaining body heat in warmer weather. In fact, you might be most comfortable if you dress in shorts and a tee shirt to shed as much excess heat as possible. In extremes of heat, however, you may find you will feel better wearing lightweight trousers and a long-sleeved shirt that provide shade from the heat of the sun.

Guidelines for Warm Weather Clothing

1. It should be thin and loose fitting to allow cooling air to circulate around your body. Remember that desert dwellers usually wear billowing robes. Loose-fitting clothing also prevents biting insects from reaching your skin.
2. Light-colored clothing reflects the sun's heat, while dark clothing absorbs sunlight and increases the chance of discomfort.
3. Your summer wardrobe should include raingear and a stocking cap since, even in desert environments known for intense heat, wind and temperature drops are not uncommon. A summer rain can make you miserably cold, as well as wet, even if the temperature stays the same.

Cold Weather Clothing

Dress in layers. To properly attire yourself for cold weather dress *not* in a heavy, dense coat but in multiple layers of loose-fitting clothing.

Undergarments

An undergarment bottom, synthetic or synthetic/wool blend, long-legged, should go on as your first bottom layer. When you wear this garment, you should wear no other underwear bottom. Some people prefer standard underwear beneath long undergarments, but if you are such a person, remember those skivvies are likely to be cotton. Take them off when you start feeling chilled. An undergarment top, synthetic or synthetic/wool blend, long-sleeved, provides the best top layer next to your

Mama Kristin Speaks

When we hit the woods, I always dress my boys in quick-drying nylon pants or shorts (available at any department or clothing store for about $10 a pair). Cotton (read: jeans) get filthy and wet, but I can rinse and hang dry the nylon jobs again and again.

skin. If the garment has a collar, you have added warmth if you need it. Tops with a zip or snap front that opens in a V allow you to partially ventilate the garment.

Mid-Layer Garments

As a mid-layer upper garment, a synthetic vest is an excellent choice. A vest adds warmth to vital body areas while allowing great ventilation and complete freedom of movement. Even with a vest, sweaters—wool or synthetic—are important mid-layer upper garments. In "warmer" cold weather, wear a light pile sweater. In colder weather, wear a heavy pile sweater in addition to the light one. Wool or synthetic trousers are best as mid-layer lower garments. Loose-fitting trousers provide more comfort and insulation and don't stick to your skin if they get damp and freeze.

Outer-Layer Garments

For an outer clothing layer, cold weather demands at least a synthetic shell that repels wet and wind from your upper and lower extremities. In intense cold, your outer layer should be insulated for maximum warmth.

Accessory Garments

A wool or synthetic cap to cover your ears and the back of your neck is a necessity. A close-knit stocking cap works well. A soft pile cap with ear flaps and a drawstring to hold it closed around your head works great. Lightweight wool or synthetic gloves are the preferred inner layer for hands. These gloves will allow the performance of some tasks, such as cooking, without exposing your hands to the cold. Wool or synthetic mittens provide the best insulation for your hands. Use mittens that fit over your gloves so you can dress your hands in layers.

Layering

Much insight lies in this simple adage: "when dressing for the cold, dress like an onion." Three lighter layers of clothing are enormously better than one heavy layer. Multiple layers, like the layers of an onion, allow you to control how much body heat and moisture you retain near your skin. Staying dry equates with staying warm, and staying warm equates with staying comfortable. When you feel yourself warming up, shed or open up a layer. When you feel yourself chilling down, add a layer. When you go shopping for clothing, you may need to buy outer garments in larger sizes so they fit over other layers.

FORGOT THE MITTENS?: If you forgot your mittens, an extra pair of wool socks substitutes in an emergency.

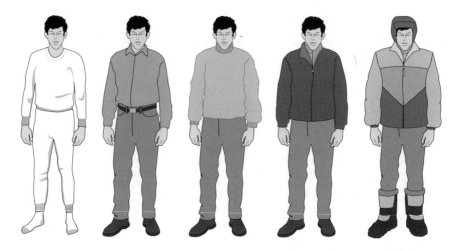

Dress like an onion.

Clothes for Cold Weather

Long undergarment top	Fleece or wool trousers
Long undergarment bottom	Stocking cap
Fleece vest	Gloves
Fleece sweater(s)	Mittens
Shell garment top	Bandanna or scarf
Shell garment bottom	

Wet Weather Clothing

You want to stay as dry as possible in warm-wet or cold-wet weather. Specifically for wet weather, you need upper—and maybe lower—garments designed to keep you dry when the clouds open up. For your upper body, a rain parka with a roomy hood is a good choice. For your lower body, rain pants do the job well. Full-leg side zippers make it easy to put on and take off pants and allow better ventilation. Half-leg zippers are almost as helpful.

TIP

PONCHOS: If you don't want to incur the expense of well-made raingear, you can get by with an inexpensive poncho, in which your head goes through a hooded hole and the garment drapes over the rest of your body. If you don't anticipate more than an occasional summer shower, you'll do fine with a poncho.

TECHNO: FABRICS

COATED NYLON: Coated nylon shells are 100 percent waterproof, and they do not "breathe," which means they allow no water to get in and no sweat to get out. You will not get wet from the rain when wearing such a shell, but you may create a sauna inside your outerwear if you are hiking up a steep trail. In an environment known for heavy rains, though, choose coated nylon rainwear.

BREATHABLE: Some synthetic shells are advertised as being waterproof and breathable at the same time. Waterproof/breathable fabrics are produced by laminating an extremely thin film onto a more durable material. The film, with millions of microscopic pores, allows tiny sweat molecules to pass through while keeping out larger water molecules, such as rain and snow. How well such materials work varies, depending on the ambient air temperature and moisture, and whether or not you have kept the fabric relatively clean. Dirt can fill the pores and prevent them from functioning. You may find these garments comfortable on a day when it is cold and dry outside. You may find yourself wet with sweat inside one of these shells when a warm rain falls on a dirty parka.

Footwear

If you plan to spend your time in camp, it doesn't matter much what you wear on your feet. You'll always want comfortable footwear and socks—and you'll want two pairs of each in case one pair gets wet or chewed to shreds by the dog in the neighboring camp. If you have out-of-camp activities planned, especially hiking, the right choice in footwear can add miles and smiles to your day.

Hiking Footwear

You can hike in any shoes, but you'll probably enjoy the experience more in thoughtfully chosen footwear. Your choices fall into one of three basic categories: lightweight "boots," midweight boots, and heavyweight boots.

- *Lightweight "boots"* look less like boots than like sport shoes made for endeavors such as tennis or basketball. With uppers typically constructed of a fabric and a flexible sole, these "boots" are designed for short trips over easy to moderate terrain while shouldering a light load.
- *Midweight boots* usually have uppers similar to lightweights, but their overall construction is heavier and their sole construction is definitely heavier. They provide enough support for longer trips over moderate terrain with a heavier load.
- *Heavyweight boots,* as the name implies, have strong rigid uppers and heavy

soles of rugged material. The sole often contains a shank, a piece of slightly flexible or nonflexible material that runs from two-thirds the length to the full length of the boot, providing security on difficult terrain. Of course they are not as comfortable as lighter boots, but you gain safety and support for your feet and ankles on tricky ground, especially if you're carrying a heavier load. Some heavyweight boots are made with plastic uppers. You see them made more often of full-grain leather that uses the entire thickness of animal hide rather than split-grain leather. Since high grades of leather are relatively waterproof and breathable, most people prefer a leather boot. Better full-grain leather boots have few seams in the uppers, and most have uppers stitched to their soles. Generally, the fewer the seams in the upper, the better the boot.

The Fit of the Boot

The single most important factor in choosing hiking footwear is the fit. Follow these guidelines when selecting a pair.

- Wear the socks you intend to hike in and lace up the boots. The second and third lacing fixtures below the top of the boot are the ones that hold your heel in place. Be sure the laces are snug there for comfort when you walk.
- Ideally, your heel should have no space for lateral movement and a minimum of up and down movement—although new boots will always allow some up and down shifting of the heel.
- The ball of your foot, at the base of your toes, should be in contact with the sides of the boot, providing a supportive pressure, not a cramped feeling.
- Along the arch of your foot, you should feel gentle contact with the boot.
- From the ball forward, there should be lessening contact, and your toes will be most content if they can wiggle freely.
- Test the fit by pressing your booted foot firmly against a wall, checking to see if the contact points remain relatively constant and if your toes stay free. Do not kick the wall and do not grind out a few deep knee bends to check a fit, both of which are unrealistic and unenlightening actions.

BREAK-IN TIME FOR BOOTS: To ease the complaints of poorly fitted feet, understand the critical importance of break-in time required for your personal flex patterns to develop in new boots. For the first week, wear your boots around the house or on short evening walks. By the end of the first week, you should be able to wear the boots all day, but keep wearing them around town for a second week before hitting the trail under a pack.

SOCK IT TO ME: For maximum comfort and protection while hiking, wear two pairs of socks: a "sock system." The keys to a successful sock system are motion between socks, the transfer of moisture, and the ability to stave off the environment. Lightweight liner socks, wool or synthetic, create a "lubricating" layer that transfers friction away from your feet to help prevent blisters. They also transfer moisture from your feet into outer socks to help keep your feet dry. Heavyweight outer socks, wool or synthetic, provide insulation and comfort. Hikers should give special attention to padding in key areas, ball and heel, where impact is greatest. And, of course, make sure the sock fits: your toes and heel should match the toe cup and heel cup of the sock.

Memories: Words and Pictures

Who you are is largely a result of what you remember.

Take a journal. All you need is an inexpensive, spiral-bound notebook. You *will* want to write down some things: details of the campground, reminders for the next trip, names and addresses of neighboring campers and, of course, those experiences too rich to trust entirely to your brain. You don't have to be as ponderous as Henry David Thoreau, as eloquent as Barry Lopez, or as irreverent as Edward Abbey—but you will want to record the adventure.

Take a camera. If you're already a photographer, you'll have your own gear, but the camera can be as unsophisticated as those ubiquitous little disposable models. If you have children, give them each a disposable camera, and encourage them to record anything they want to see again. Snapshots of your people at the campsite doing their thing will encourage the wonderful memories to flow and delight.

Bits and Pieces

In addition to the "big" stuff—tent, bags, kitchen gear, clothes—you'll want to have a number of smaller items with you.

Tables

Many campground sites provide a picnic table, which can be an excellent place to set your stove, prepare your food, set out your plates and cups, and enjoy your meals. If you have chosen a campground without tables, consider bringing one—just a small, collapsible model. If it folds out into a 4-x-4-foot surface, stands 2 feet off the ground, and folds into a tube for easy packing, it will be fine. You will appreciate the convenience very much.

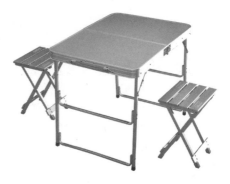

Almost all the comforts of a dining room at home.

A chair can add a lot to camp comfort.

Chairs

Camp chairs will add much to camp comfort when it's time to sip hot chocolate, chat, watch the sunset, or observe the fire as it dies to red coals. Inexpensive folding chairs, a soft fabric sewn to a collapsible frame, will serve well, and they can be purchased—if you keep an eye peeled for sales—for as little as $5. You can spend more for folding camp chairs that recline or for those that offer extras, such as cup holders and footrests.

First-Aid Kit

Every camp needs a first-aid kit. You may not use it during your first trip, or your second, but you *will* use it. Excellent outdoor first-aid kits are available commercially, and one made for the outdoors is definitely the way to go. Atwater Carey, for example, makes great kits for campers.

First-Aid Kit Guidelines

There's no such thing as a perfect first-aid kit. Eventually, if you spend enough time camping, you will one day wish for something that just isn't there, and you might find yourself willing to trade your sleeping bag for a glob of itch-soothing calamine lotion.

Kits become personal. You may find blisters forming on your feet if you walk across a parking lot, but your camping companions have feet of steel. The following can help you decide what to put in your kit:

1. *Evaluate your kit after every trip.* Check any medications in your kit, and replace the ones that have reached their expiration dates. Also pack a few of the common over-the-counter drugs, such as ibuprofen, antacid tablets, and a diarrhea medication, and perhaps an antihistamine and a decongestant spray. If you're camping with your kids, remember to bring child-strength medications. Be sure to pack any medications that have been prescribed or recommended by a physician for you or members of your family. Check the

adhesive strips and gauze in your kit, and make sure they have not been damaged by moisture. Replace the items you have used, and add items you wish you'd had on your last trip.

2. *When you add items to your kit, be sure you know how to use them.* You may be enticed to purchase a suture kit, but unless you're professionally trained to sew up wounds, attempting to suture will be inappropriate at best and dangerous at worst. Even simple bandaging materials work effectively if applied correctly.

3. *Because you want to be ready to give the best care possible, take a first-aid and a CPR course.* Better yet, take a wilderness first-aid course. Such courses are designed to meet immediate medical needs, but they also prepare you to provide care over long periods of time, a possibility you might face if you camp far from help. If a serious accident occurs, human life and limb are not saved by items stuffed in a kit but by knowledge carried in your brain.

4. *Even if you take a course, it's a great idea to carry a small first-aid guide.* You probably won't remember everything you learned in class (see Chapter 8).

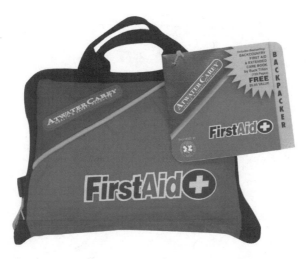

Much better to have it and not need it than to need it and not have it.

Lantern

After sunset, you might want to cook, clean, read, write, or maybe even set camp. You'll want to illuminate the darkness, and no matter how big and bright your fire, you'll want a lantern. As with stoves, you'll have quite a few choices in lanterns. They come small and large and in between, and they come powered by batteries, gas in a cartridge (propane, butane), or liquid fuel (white gas, unleaded fuel).

A *battery-powered lantern* is the simplest but often the most expensive to operate due to the cost of batteries. On one end of the spectrum of battery-powered lanterns, you will find inexpensive models that are little more than large flashlights. On the other end, you will find virtual floodlights, some available with remote controls that allow you to turn the lantern on from a distance so its light can guide you back to your tent in the dark.

A *propane or butane lantern* burns, you guessed it, propane or butane—or a mixture of both—and has a fuel cartridge that attaches to the lantern. When the cartridge is empty, you simply unscrew it and screw on a fresh one. These lanterns are safe and efficient—no pouring of fuel, no pumping—but they're more expensive to run than liquid-fuel lanterns. The length of time you'll get light depends on the size of the cartridge and how high you turn the light. Speaking of turning up the light, some propane lanterns will brighten an entire campsite on high but can be turned down to a soft glow to illuminate a quiet dinner.

A *liquid-fuel lantern* requires you to fill the lantern's tank, pump up the pressure, and either strike a match or flick the switch on an electric-ignition model. Small liquid-fuel lanterns will burn three hours or so on high before a refill is

A bright idea from Coleman

needed. Large lanterns will burn seven hours or more on high. They also burn the fuel as it vaporizes around a mantle. The mantle has to be replaced periodically. Refilling and mantle replacement are a bother, but not a big one, and liquid fuel is inexpensive: a gallon will last you many camping trips.

Flashlights

Choices in flashlights are too numerous to consider in depth here. You can find small flashlights with amazingly bright light, so you don't have to buy a big light to get a big light. Choose a flashlight that uses standard batteries and standard bulbs. It will be much easier to find replacements, but carry extra batteries and bulbs in case you need them in the middle of the night.

HEADLAMPS: Consider using a headlamp, which is like a flashlight with a band allowing it to be worn on your forehead. If you need your hands free for nighttime chores, you'll appreciate a headlamp for its hands-free operation.

CARRY A FUNNEL: If you're packing stoves and lanterns that run on liquid fuel, carry a small funnel. Pouring fuel will be much easier, and you'll waste less of it.

Saw

You can get along without a saw, but a small folding saw can be extremely useful in cutting firewood. It's easy to use, and it's safe to carry if you choose one with a blade that folds into the handle.

Hatchet

You can get along without a hatchet, but there will be times when firewood works better if you split it first (see Chapter 6). Hatchets are handy when you need to drive tent stakes into hard ground. Choose a hatchet with a cover that protects the blade edge when not in use—and protects you and your vehicle when you pack it.

Shovel

A small shovel might get a lot of use: moving coals around the campfire for cooking (see Chapter 7), digging the refuse of untidy campers out of a fireplace,

Mama Kristin Speaks

Equip each kid with a mini flashlight attached to a lanyard necklace. The lights are great for getting around camp at night, as well as for creating laser shows and shadow-puppet plays in the tent.

digging cat holes and fire pits at remote camping sites (see Chapter 10)—and who knows what else.

Repair Kits

No matter how durable your gear or clothing, you should anticipate the possibility that something may fall apart, burst open, or rip. To be prepared, pack a small repair kit. The contents of your repair kit will depend, to some degree, on your specific camping gear. Your stove, your sleeping pad, and your lantern, for example, may come with a set of items that allow you to perform simple repair jobs in camp. I have a small stuff sack designated as my repair kit, and into this go all the little repair kits that came with my gear. If I need to repair something, it's all there in one place. Here are a few more thoughts:

- *Duct tape.* If it can't be fixed with duct tape, it probably can't be fixed in camp. There are exceptions, of course, but pack the duct tape.
- *Mechanical wire and a small pair of pliers.* A short piece of wire and a quick twist with the pliers can temporarily reattach things that are supposed to stay attached on their own.
- *Sewing kit.* A small one allows quick stitching up of torn clothing.
- *Parachute cord.* A piece twenty or so feet long almost always seems to come in handy for emergencies such as to replace broken bootlaces or to add additional tent tie-downs if the wind kicks up.

Packing Your Vehicle

A little thoughtful attention here can simplify camp setup (see Chapter 4).

1. *Put the stuff you'll want first in your vehicle last.* If you like to pitch the tent as soon as possible, for example, put the tent in your vehicle last. Keep the first-aid kit and a roll of toilet paper handy. You probably won't mind burying the kitchen gear.

2. *Make use of two or three large, inexpensive, plastic storage bins*—the ones with snug-fitting lids. Anything that uses fuel can go in one, including the fuel. If fuel spills in your vehicle, it gets caught, saving the vehicle and keeping the odor of fuel out of the vehicle. You can use another one for storage of food that doesn't need to be kept chilled. Side by side in camp, the cooler and the food bin become refrigerator and cupboard. They keep stuff organized, and they fit neatly in your vehicle.

3. *Save room inside your vehicle by using a car-top carrier.* None of them are remarkably easy to load and unload, but they do extend the carrying capacity of your vehicle quite a bit. Large, box-shaped carriers hold a mound of gear, but their shape creates a lot of wind resistance when you're traveling. Long, lean carriers, designed to shed wind (the type that attaches to a roof rack), work well aerodynamically, but they don't hold as much. If you choose a car-top carrier, you'll appreciate the security of one that locks.

4. *Pack clothing in a large zippered duffel bag.* If the zipper runs the length of the bag, it's easy to access accessing shirts and jackets. The bag itself should be highly water resistant, enough so that there are no worries about setting it on damp ground or having a bit of rain fall on it. Without a duffel bag, you can carry clothes in a plastic garbage bag. It's more difficult to access what you want, but everything stays dry.

5. *If you plan specific camp activities, such as biking or canoeing* (see Chapter 9), you may be able to rent the bike or canoe at the campground. If you carry your own, you'll need a roof rack for the top of your vehicle. Some roof racks allow you to strap down a canoe or sea kayak, and some offer removable adapters made specifically for carrying bicycles.

A MASTER CHECKLIST: There's a lot to remember, so don't try. Create a checklist of all the items you want to take along—or use the one included as Appendix D in this book.

"Primitive" campsites may require you to collect and filter your water.

GOING—WHERE AND WHEN

Maybe you know exactly where you'd like to set camp. You've heard great things about a certain campground, or it's relatively nearby, or it's close to attractions you've long wanted to visit. You might have generated a list of the places you want to camp—a dream list—and you're ready to start making those dreams come true. Or maybe you're sold on the idea of camping, but you don't know where you want to go. In this chapter you'll find general suggestions about where to go—and when—and how to find specific information about specific campgrounds and other possible places to pitch your tent.

{ **In the Words of a Sage** }

Silence and seclusion are the secrets of success. In this modern life of activity there is only one way to separate yourself from its ceaseless demands: get away from it once in a while.
—*Paramahansa Yogananda*

Where to Go

Federal public lands in the United States encompass a total of approximately 730 million acres, and you can find a huge number of campgrounds among those acres. Add in the thousands of established campsites on state-owned recreation acres, and the number of camping possibilities grows massively larger. And then

North America offers the opportunity to set a camp in more than 10,000 privately owned campgrounds. All these campgrounds, however, are not created equal. Depending on the government agency or the private campground owner who manages the campgrounds, you will find differences, sometimes big differences, in amenities, rules, restrictions, and reservation policies.

Just the Facts: Campgrounds at a Glance

	Number	Fees	Access	Amenities	Reservations
National Park Service (NPS)	440	Yes	Pavement	Full	Recommended
U.S. Forest Service (USFS)	4300+	Sometimes	Dirt	Variable	Variable
Bureau of Land Management (BLM)	400+	Sometimes	Dirt	Primitive	No
U.S. Fish & Wildlife Service (USF&WS)	Few	Sometimes	Variable	Variable	Yes
State	1000s	Sometimes	Pavement	Variable	Recommended
Private	10,000+	Yes	Pavement	Variable	Recommended

There are thousands and thousands of campsites to choose from on public and private land.

National Park Campgrounds

The National Park Service (NPS) manages land totaling about 80 million acres. It's a staggering diversity of land: parks, monuments, battlefields, lakeshores, seashores, historic sites, memorials, and rivers. Camping is not allowed on a lot of NPS land, but more than a hundred national parks and monuments do allow it. Approximately 440 National Park Service campgrounds are set on some of the best land in North America, and all are accessible on well-maintained, paved roads. The campgrounds almost always have drinking water, picnic tables, fire rings, and rest rooms, and some have hot showers. Because the NPS is charged with preserving public lands not only for our enjoyment but for future generations as well, you'll find more use restrictions at NPS campgrounds than on other federal lands, such as trails closed to mountain bikes, dogs allowed only on leashes (or not at all), and areas closed to the gathering of firewood.

The NPS charges an entry fee to visitors, even if you don't plan to camp. If more than a couple of parks are on your camping agenda, you'll do well to purchase a National Park Service Pass for $50. The pass will allow you, and almost always everybody in your vehicle, into all the national parks for one year. The pass is available online at all national parks where an entry fee is charged, as well as by calling 1-888-GOPARKS. Once inside a park, you'll pay another fee—typically between $10 and $16 per night—for a campsite. *Be warned:* NPS campgrounds

The National Park Service preserves some of the best of America.

are extremely popular, especially in the summer and over holidays. Some sites are available on a first-come, first-served basis, but reservations are often accepted and strongly recommended (see "Information and Reservations").

You can find information about all the campgrounds in the book *National Park Service Camping Guide,* which you can order online. You can also go to the National Park Service website and click on the park that interests you.

TIP

VISITOR CENTERS: If the park you're visiting has a visitor center, make it your first stop. You'll find detailed information—from the staff, from exhibits, from brochures—about the campgrounds and the park itself, including attractions, activities, natural history, and human history.

Just the Facts: VIPs

In fiscal year 2004, more than 140,000 volunteers donated time and energy to help make the National Park System better able to serve the public. Volunteers-in-Parks *(www.nps.gov/volunteer)* worked a total of more than 5 million hours. You too can help.

Forest Service Campgrounds

The United States Forest Service (USFS) manages approximately 193 million acres of forests and grasslands, a total land mass about the same size as Texas. On USFS land, you'll find more than 4300 campgrounds—and, generally speaking, the campgrounds are less developed than NPS campgrounds. You'll usually find water and rest rooms, or at least pit toilets, but you'll seldom find hot showers. Sometimes you'll find little more than a clear spot to camp and a fire ring. Access is typically on a graded dirt road. Fewer restrictions govern Forest Service campgrounds. No nationwide USFS campground rules apply, so the only way to know if any restrictions are in force is to check with the specific national forest you want to visit.

Sometimes a fee is required, and sometimes not. Sometimes the campgrounds are staffed by a manager, and sometimes not. You can find information about each and every one of these campgrounds in the *National Forest Campground and Recreation Directory.* Enter the book's name into an online search engine, and you'll be given several sources for placing an order. Many USFS campgrounds accept reservations (see "Information and Reservations").

Bureau of Land Management Campgrounds

The Bureau of Land Management (BLM) manages more than 261 million acres of national public land in the United States, almost all of it in the eleven contiguous western states and Alaska. On BLM land you'll find more than 400 campgrounds and approximately 17,000 campsites. Most of the campsites are primitive: a clearing, a picnic table, a fire ring—sometimes a rest room. Access may be primitive as well—a long, dusty, bumpy road. Seldom will you find an on-site manager. The campgrounds are typically either free or "managed" by an "iron ranger," a metal box into which you'll put a fee rarely varying from a range of $5 to $10 per night. Most of the campsites are open on a first-come, first-served basis, and reservations are almost never required or accepted. You can read all about the campgrounds online (see "Information and Reservations"), and you can also find information at the BLM website.

U.S. Fish & Wildlife Service Campgrounds

The U.S. Fish & Wildlife Service (USF&WS) manages land on 476 preserves set aside for the protection of critical habitat for birds and other wildlife species. USF&WS land is almost always near waterways or wetlands, and most areas do not allow camping. The areas that do allow camping offer excellent wildlife viewing opportunities, and often great hiking or paddling. You can find out about the areas and the camping possibilities at the USF&WS website.

State Park and Forest Campgrounds

An inventory of state parks, preserves, and forests in the United States includes more than 5000 areas. The variety of areas is immense, and the sites are often magnificent, but not all these areas offer campgrounds. The inventory does include a total of more than 74,000 "improved" year-round campsites and more than 72,000 "improved" seasonal (closed in winter) campsites for a grand total of more than 146,000 "improved" campsites, the great majority of them in the eastern United States. Access is usually on a paved road, and, all things considered, state campgrounds tend to be more developed than federal campgrounds. You'll find water, grills, picnic tables, rest rooms, and sometimes electricity and showers. If you're willing to rough it, you'll also find more than 49,000 "primitive" campsites—those without amenities—in the state parks of the United States. With a grand total of almost 200,000 campsites on state-managed land, you're sure to find quite a few places where you'll love to set up camp. Some of these campgrounds demand a fee, and some don't. Some strongly recommend reservations (see "Information and Reservations").

Private Campgrounds

Unlike campgrounds on state and national public land, private campgrounds are businesses, managed to make a profit and quite varied in terms of rules and regulations. Private campgrounds are set on private land, sometimes far from the wild and beautiful landscapes you want to see when you camp. They are more often than not built to accept RVs, and some of them have no tent sites. On the other hand, you will undoubtedly find some of these places tremendously appealing. You can find excellent private campgrounds with outstanding amenities that are well managed, and you can find unattractive private campgrounds with poor management. The best way to find out specifics is to talk with someone who has camped in one of these places. Expect to pay more, often a lot more, to camp in private campgrounds, sometimes as much or more than a motel room.

TIP

INFORMATION AND RESERVATIONS: At *www.recreation.gov,* you'll find information, often including directions, about NPS, USFS, and BLM campgrounds, and you can make reservations for NPS and USFS campsites. You'll find data for 1547 campgrounds at this site.

Go to *www.nationalparksociety.com* to obtain a copy of the *National Park Service Camping Guide* or to *us-national-parks.net* for further information.

For information on specific USFS campgrounds, go to *www.fs.fed.us,* or obtain a copy of the *National Forest Campground and Recreation Directory* at *www.recreation.gov* or *www.amazon.com.*

For information about BLM lands, go to *www.blm.gov,* and for USF&WS info, go to *www.fws.gov.*

You can obtain a directory of state offices that manage state park land at *usparks.about.com.*

You will find information about more than 10,000 private campgrounds in the United States and Canada at *www.bisdirectory.com.*

Just the Facts: Choosing a Campground

- If the campground is publicized as an RV park, you'll do best to avoid the place. If it isn't labeled as one, but if the campground offers lots of "hookups" and "dumping stations" for RVs, it's probably best to avoid that one, too. It's difficult to appreciate a campsite between towering metal, wheeled homes with rattling generators, and TV's blaring.
- If the campground offers a section reserved for "tents only," it's likely you'll find a site with at least a bit of privacy and seclusion.
- If the campground provides more than a hundred campsites, you'll probably have close neighbors, and some of them are likely to be noisy. Campgrounds with fifty or fewer sites will give you a better chance for peace and quiet. I've found that the smaller the campground, the better I like it—but that's just me.
- If the campground provides buffers between sites—rocks, bushes, trees—you'll more than likely enjoy the site more. "Wooded" sites usually give you plenty of buffers. "Open" sites usually means just that: no buffers. "Semi-open" sites could be anything.

Finding Your Own Spot

On most USFS and BLM land, you're allowed to set a camp anywhere that isn't posted with signs saying you can't. You can park your vehicle in clearings near logging roads and access roads, not far from rivers, lakes, and seashores, or up against the broad expanses of mountain meadows. You'll often find spots that have appealed to previous campers, with tent sites flattened by use and fire rings composed of stones. Sometimes ideal-looking campsites are on private land, and the owner may or may not be willing to allow you to camp. It is your responsibility to learn if land is public or private, and to politely approach the owner of private land to ask whether or not camping is allowed. Setting a primitive camp all on your own has tremendous appeal to many people, but more will be required of you (see Chapter 10).

When to Go

Whether you're anticipating a weekend getaway or a week-long vacation, the time of year you choose to go can add—or subtract—from your experience.

Summer. Summer is, as you know, the vacation season in the United States, especially July and August. It's a good season to avoid the country's main attractions: the big national and state parks and other popular destinations. Look instead at out-of-the-way campgrounds where you can find more silence and seclusion, or plan your trip in spring or fall before the vacation rush. If you're unsure about a spot's popularity, contact the land management agency for the area you're thinking about visiting.

Holidays. Holidays are another time of year to think about the less-visited campgrounds. You probably don't want to end up next to a dozen rampaging college students during spring break or crammed into a small site near a hundred other tents on the Fourth of July.

Environmental Conditions. You also want to consider the environmental conditions. Joshua Tree National Park in southern California, for example, typically heats up like a furnace in midsummer, but the area can be splendidly appealing in late fall. Rocky Mountain National Park in Colorado may be under snow in early summer, but the same area offers perfect camping weather in late summer. Once again, a call to the land management agency or an online check is strongly recommended.

Camp setup is a process.

4

CAMP SETUP

When you pull your vehicle into your chosen campground (see Chapter 3), you're almost ready to start setting up camp. Camp setup is a process—a wonderful process—of putting each and every piece of gear in just the right spot for the ultimate camping experience. Once camp is set to your satisfaction, the pursuit of life in camp continues: the cooking, the cleaning, the sleeping, as well as the other activities you choose to make a part of your camping life (see Chapter 9). This chapter is about the basics of life in camp.

{ **In the Words of a Sage** }

And there at the camp we had around us the elemental world of water and light, and earth and air. We felt the presences of the wild creatures, the river, the trees, the stars. Though we had our troubles, we had them in a true perspective.

—*Wendell Berry*

Campsite Selection

Before you begin setting up your camp, you'll have to choose a site within the campground. Your choice can add or subtract a lot from your experience.

- *Choose early.* Because you want the best site, arrive at the campground, if possible, before noon, when other campers are heading out and new campers have yet to arrive in an afternoon mass, before you're stuck with what's left. In many popular campgrounds, the prime sites are usually all taken long before 4:00 PM.

- *Did you make a reservation?* In some popular campgrounds managed by state or national agencies, arriving early may not matter even if you have a reservation since someone in a uniform could greet you at the entrance and provide you with directions to an assigned campsite. In such an instance, however, if you don't like the site—and if you arrived early, and if you're nice—you may be able to talk the staff into changing your assigned site.
- *Check for "tents only" sites.* In some campgrounds, you'll find an area set aside for tents only. You may not be required to camp there, but it's not a bad idea. It keeps you away from large recreational vehicles (RVs) and their nightlong clatter of generators. A more natural setting is often found in tents-only areas—more trees, more picturesque rocks, a better view of the landscape.
- *Avoid high-traffic areas.* Although it might seem handy to set camp near a rest room or bathhouse, you probably don't want to do that. There may be lights shining from the rest room all through the dark hours, and you can be awakened by slamming doors in the middle of the best sleep you've ever had. On the other hand, you may choose to camp near a rest room if you have small children along. Avoid sites near the entrance to the campground where traffic also tends to be heavy.
- *Look for "buffers."* Buffers are trees and bushes, perhaps large rocks, standing between campsites. They'll give you more privacy and a greater sense of seclusion.

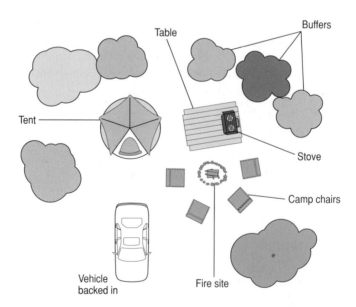

The anatomy of a campsite

Consider heading first for the back of a campground. Even without buffers, those sites tend to provide more privacy.

- *Look for shade and sunlight.* It's great to find a site that gives you shade in summer and sunlight during the colder months. You won't always find it, but, again, it's great if you do.

BACK IT IN: When you've chosen a site, back your vehicle into the parking space. You will have a bit more privacy, and the gear you unload and later load will be more accessible.

THE VALUE OF EXPERIENCE: If you're new to camping, go the first time with someone experienced. A great deal of wisdom can be gained from experienced campers, and you won't have to learn all your lessons the hard way. You may also check with local parks and recreation departments. You can often find clinics that are offered for novice campers.

Tent Site Selection

Many campgrounds will have a tent site waiting for you: a flat spot, firmly packed, ready for your dome away from home. If you have to choose your own tent site, find a level spot. Remember that the tent site may only *look* level.

- To be sure a tent site is level, lie on the ground, or on the tent before it is set up, approximately where you think your sleeping bag will be. If you find your

Once it's set, camp is your home away from home.

head slightly elevated, that's okay, but you don't want your feet higher than your head.

- Choose a sleeping arrangement that puts no one at a sideways angle on the ground. Tilted sideways, you'll sleep less well, and you may slip off your pad during the night.
- If you find small depressions in the ground on which your tent will stand, you may be able to fill them with pine needles or leaves to create a flatter surface.
- Avoid setting your tent in a low spot where water will collect in a rain. You don't want to wake up in the middle of a small pond, so check the spot carefully, even if it appears to be flat.
- The tent site should be free of obstacles such as small rocks, pine cones, twigs, and such, all of which can be moved. Large, half-buried rocks cannot be moved, and neither can tree roots.

Pitching Your Tent

No two tents pitch exactly the same, but, generally speaking, you'll spread the tent out flat on your chosen site, assemble the poles, and set the poles in their predetermined places. The tent will pop up as you flex the poles and set the ends in grommets, or you'll have to lift and attach the tent to the poles with clips. If you have a fly, it will go on last.

THE FIRST PITCH: If you purchase your tent from an outdoor specialty store, a clerk will be willing to show you how to set it up. Even though all tents come with pitching instructions, watch the clerk do it the first time, and pay close attention. Then do it again at home, on your own, before taking it camping.

If you purchase your tent from a large discount store, the clerk probably has no idea how to set it up. You'll be on your own from the first pitch. Then it becomes even more important to set it up a couple of times at home before heading for your chosen campsite. If you have trouble pitching a tent at home, it will *not* be easier in camp.

STAKING THE TENT: Some tent manufacturers, depending on the style of tent, suggest staking it out before setting the poles in place, and others suggest the opposite. With a dome-shaped tent, set the poles first and wait to set the stakes. This will allow you to shift the tent around, if you need to, before staking it out. In an ideal situation, you can push the stakes into firm ground with your hands. If the ground is hard, you can pound them in, but do so gently because you can bend metal stakes and break plastic ones. Don't bury the stakes too deeply, just deeply enough to secure the tent. Remember: you will eventually have to pull them out.

Heating the Tent

Some campers are drawn to campsites in cold weather. There are wonders in every season, and winter holds its own special charms. With a dense pad and a fluffy bag, you'll have a sound night's sleep when the mercury drops, but at some point you'll have to crawl out of that warm bag. You may be tempted, therefore, to bring a source of heat into your tent. The basic rule is this: *don't do it!* Get up and get moving to create heat inside your body, or get up and build a roaring fire to create heat outside your body. Campers who have experimented with various sources of heating a tent seldom report success, and some have failed to report at all—because they died from carbon monoxide poisoning or because the tent erupted in flames.

There are two *possible* exceptions. Campsites with electricity may offer the opportunity to use an electric heater, and gas catalytic heaters may *possibly* be safe to use. Gas catalytic heaters utilize propane without an open flame. Even though exceptions can be found, your safest bet is to buy a fluffier sleeping bag and leave the heaters at home.

The Ironclad Rules for Heating a Tent

Tent heaters come with several rules that must *never* be broken:

1. *Never* set a tent heater directly on the tent's floor.
2. *Never* use a tent heater without adequate ventilation.
3. *Never* place anything within two feet of a tent heater.
4. *Never* sleep with a heater turned on.

Making the Bed

With your tent pitched, lay out your sleeping pads. If they need to be blown up, go ahead and do it. Don't wait until dark. Lie on your pad, making sure it's oriented properly and that you didn't miss a rock that ended up beneath your shoulder. Pull your sleeping bags out of their stuff sacks and spread them on the pads. They'll fluff up and be ready when sleep beckons.

- When bedtime arrives, any clothing you choose to sleep in should be dry. Don't sack out, for example, in a tee shirt damp with sweat from the day's activities. Damp clothing at best will cause discomfort. At worst, it'll chill you during a cool night.

- Always sleep with the tent door and a window partially open to allow air to flow through. Without ventilation, the moisture released by sleeping bodies can dampen the inside of the tent and everything else inside. In humid weather, keep the doors and windows open all the way—and keep the mosquito netting zipped shut. Humidity requires a lot of ventilation if you want to awake dry.

- Keep a stocking cap near you in the tent. If you wake up chilled, a cap often adds enough warmth to chase away the chill.

- Fall asleep with a full water bottle handy to deal with a sudden middle-of-the-night thirst. Better to get up and urinate than to sleep dehydrated.

- Place footwear under the tent's vestibule or just inside the tent door to keep it dry and handy. If you need to slip out of the tent during the night, slip into your footwear. It is *not* a good idea to walk around camp barefoot in the dark.

- In fact, it's not a good idea to walk around in the dark, so keep a flashlight in the tent. Even if you don't need to leave the tent, a light might come in handy when you need to find something in the dark.

- In the morning, after a refreshing night's sleep, turn your sleeping bags inside out and hang them outside, over a line or the top of the tent, for a half hour or so. They'll be dry and ready for the next night, or dry and ready to be stuffed back into their sacks.

- You can hang wet clothing outside during the day. Hanging damp clothes outside the tent may work at night, but it may not, so at night hang damp clothing on a clothesline you've strung high inside the tent. You don't want to wake up to even damper clothes if a rain or heavy dew falls.

- Develop the habit of always wearing a soft, comfortable pair of shoes around camp. Your feet will be not only comfy but also protected from sharp objects carelessly left by other campers, protected from thorns and burrs, and protected from stray embers from the fire. You will also create less impact on the land with soft-soled shoes.

A tent is the place to sleep or play.

Camp Kitchen Setup

Designate an area of the campsite as the kitchen. This area should not be littered with other camping stuff. Muddy boots, sleeping bags, and stuffed animals will get in the way and become a source of irritation. A picnic table is an obvious choice. You can set the stove on one end and spread the food waiting for preparation across its broad surface. You can set up the washtub on the other end. Filled with water, the washtub will be ready for soaking food scraps off pots and dishes as soon as you are done using them. If you're cooking on a portable camp table, set it out of the camp's traffic patterns. You will have enough distractions during meal preparation (see Chapter 7) without folks walking between the cook and the stove on their way to the bathroom or the tent.

THE CAMP COOK: A head camp cook is a good idea, and it's a great idea when someone enjoys cooking—especially when that someone does it well. If you're the cook, don't get stuck in the kitchen by yourself. Organize the group and give assignments. For example, someone can cut veggies while someone else gets water. You especially don't want to be alone at cleanup time!

TIP

Camp Kitchen Cleanup

- After eating, if you haven't caught and/or picked up every last crumb and tossed them into a garbage bag or the fire, do it now. Don't burn leftover food. It doesn't work. Pack it all out. And never bury leftovers: animals will dig them up.
- If you've used pots or pans, clean them right away. The longer you wait, the more aggressively food sticks to the cooking surface. A little thinking ahead will go a long way here. Put a pot of water over the coals of the fire or on the stove while you're enjoying dinner. With hot water and a scrubbing sponge, you'll soon have the pots, cups, spoons, and other cooking paraphernalia spotless.
- Do not toss the "gray water"—the water filled with food scraps and soap— into the forest where it pollutes the environment and attracts animals. Never toss gray water into rivers, lakes, or other water sources. Small splashes of gray water can be tossed in the fire. Large amounts should be poured into the dump stations you'll find at many campgrounds. If you don't have access to a dump station, pour the dirty water through a small strainer, a coffee filter, or even a bandanna, and throw the scraps into the campground's trash bin or pack them out in your garbage bag. With the scraps removed, you can broadcast the remaining water across a grassy area well away from campsites.

Camp Hygiene

It's a microscopic jungle out there, full of germs looking for a host—and you are decidedly host material. Poor camp hygiene remains the leading cause of illness in campers. Here are five of the most important things you can do to stay healthy:

1. *Wash your hands after using the toilet and before preparing or eating food.* Nothing, absolutely nothing, maintains hygiene better than clean hands. Research indicates the washing method that works best: wet your hands with hot water. Lather up with any soap. Work the lather into your hands, concentrating on your fingertips. Scrub for thirty seconds. Rinse with hot water. Dry your hands with a clean paper or cloth towel. *Remember:* any method of hand washing beats the heck out of *no* hand washing.

2. *Save time and energy with a hand sanitizer.* The alcohol in many hand sanitizers, which you can purchase in stores everywhere, is a mighty germ killer. In some tests, hands actually ended up more

Mama Kristin Speaks

Recruit young helpers for dish duty. That basin of warm soapy water not only cleans your cooking gear. It's also a great opportunity to scrub little hands at the end of a dirty day.

germ free than when they were washed (see "Hand Sanitization").

3. *Care, but don't share.* Other than terrorists, no one passes around germs intentionally, but a multitude of microscopic critters are thoughtlessly shared (see "Care, Don't Share")

4. *Wash dishes, cups, and eating utensils every day.* Pots and pans brought to high heat during food prep can go for several days between washings. Follow these recommendations:

   a. Remove as much of the visible food scraps as possible.

   b. Use hot, soapy water and an abrasive pad.

   c. Rinse with hot water and wipe dry with a clean paper or cloth towel, or rinse in cold water with chlorine added. (It doesn't take much chlorine. If the water smells faintly of chlorine, there's enough in there.)

5. *If you can't refrigerate leftovers, don't eat them.* Germs proliferate in old, cooked food.

HAND SANITIZATION:

- Make sure alcohol is the active ingredient.
- Follow the directions on the label.
- Choose a hand sanitizer with added moisturizer to counteract the drying effect of alcohol.
- Once a day wash your hands the old-fashioned way to get rid of the grime sanitizers don't remove.

TIPS

CARE, DON'T SHARE:

- Do not reach into the snack bag. Shake the yummies out into your hand.
- Do not drink from someone else's cup or water bottle, or use their un-washed spoon.
- Do not share your napkin or bandanna.
- Do not let someone else finish your half-eaten granola bar.

KEEPING KIDS CLEAN: If you have kids in camp, which is always a treasured experience, and if the campground has rest rooms with sinks, re-mind the kids to wash their hands after going to the bathroom. Without sinks with running water, warm up enough water, on a stove or over a fire, so they can "clean off the night" before breakfast. There's something about clean hands and a clean face—no exceptions—that makes life a bit sweeter. *And, remember:* clean hands do much to keep germs out of intestinal tracts.

Critter-Free Campsites

Psychologists might call it an approach-avoidance conflict. Gosh, those little crit-ters are cute, and seeing them adds a heap of fun to the camping experience—and

This cute little guy is waiting for a snack you do *not* want to provide.

you want them to approach. But then the squirrels gnaw into the bag of nuts, the raccoon learns to crack the combination on the cooler, and the skunk sprays little Timmy—and you want to avoid them. No matter what precautions you take, you can't keep all the pesky wild things away all the time, but you can take steps to reduce the possibility of a successful fur-clad raid on your campsite.

1. *Do not feed the animals.* As irresistible as that fuzzy face might be, resist. Do not intentionally drop a food scrap to attract the watchful chipmunk. Do not attempt to feed animals with food from your hand. If they learn to accept handheld food, they are only a nip away from biting the hand that feeds them. A bite may be serious immediately from the damage and later from the germs in the animal's mouth.

2. *Keep your camp clean.* Do not unintentionally feed wildlife by failing to pick up every scrap of food, every empty container, and any trash lying anywhere. An unnoticed potato chip can become an unwholesome snack for quick-footed camp raiders moments after it hits the ground.

3. *Store food in the vehicle.* Food stored behind glass and steel will be inaccessible to wild animals—with, perhaps, one exception: a mighty hungry and none-too-small bear. Habituated bears have been known to break out vehicle windows to get at tasty treats. If bears are that much of a threat, the campground will usually make you aware of it with signs and/or warnings from site managers. The campground may provide bear-proof storage containers. If it doesn't, hide the food you store in your vehicle. Coolers under blankets in backseats and food boxes in vehicle trunks are seldom assaulted by

bears. If they can't see it, in other words, they're less likely to go for it.

4. *Do not tempt animals.* Odors may attract animals from surprisingly great distances—especially some specific odors, and especially bears. Bacon or fish frying on a stove, for example, is enormously enticing. If you catch fresh fish, never clean them near your camp. Wash and store your used cookware and utensils as soon as possible to remove odors. Sugary foods are temptations to animals large and small. Toothpaste and sweet-smelling toiletries will also attract some animals. Be sure to store anything aromatic in your vehicle. Animals are attracted, as well, to salt and salt-laden products. Carry them, but don't leave them lying around. Even urine and fecal matter will tempt some animals into camp. If the campground has a rest room, use it.

5. *Properly dispose of all garbage.* Many campgrounds have dumpsters or special garbage cans, and all your garbage should go where it's supposed to go. If no appropriate receptacles are available for your garbage, bag it, store it in your vehicle, and dispose of it properly later.

KILLING WITH KINDNESS: Wild animals become a problem for you, but you, unknowingly, might be an even greater problem for them. Animals that become dependent on campground grub—that is, the ones that become habituated—are often trapped and relocated or, in extreme circumstances, exterminated.

Campground Etiquette

It's unlikely you'll have a campground all to yourself. Others will have made their plans, packed their gear, and driven for hours to the same place. They, like you, will be anticipating a beautiful setting with fresh air and at least relative peace and quiet. How disappointing to finally arrive and find the campground atmosphere destroyed by other campers. A few simple guidelines, if followed, will make the campground experience richer for everyone.

1. *Appreciate and honor the boundaries of your site.* Take time with any children to make sure they understand the boundaries. Do *not* walk through the sites of other campers, even if that provides the shortest route to a rest room. This is your area, and that's their area.

2. *Introduce yourself to your neighbors.* A friendly "Hi" and exchange of names and a little personal information sets the stage for good relations. A good neighbor will keep an eye on your site when you're off hiking, and you can do the same for them. Besides, you might need to borrow a pinch of salt.

3. *If you've brought a radio or disc player, keep the volume down.* Be especially observant of quiet hours and quiet zones (radio-free zones). These times and places are almost always posted near the campground entrance.

4. *Manage your pet.* You may think your puppy is the greatest pet in the world, but your neighbors may not (see Chapter 5).

5. *Keep your campsite clean.* Trash, especially food scraps, may attract wild animals (as previously noted). Trash is also unsightly, and some of it may develop a distasteful smell. Use campground trash receptacles and recycling bins, or keep your trash in a garbage bag to be taken home.

6. *Do not wash your dishes or cookware at the campground's water source.* You don't want to keep your neighbors waiting to fill a pot while you scrub out your frying pan, and you don't want to leave messy scraps around the faucet. Do your cleaning up at your campsite.

7. *Be considerate with and around your campfire.* A huge bonfire may be fun for you, but it might be intrusive to your neighbors. If you like to sit up late around the fire, keep the noise low. Your loud talking might disturb others trying to sleep. Put out the fire before your bedtime. It might be required at the campground, and even if it's not, the smoke from a smoldering fire may drift through nearby tents.

{ Personal Reflections }

Peace reigns more at dawn than at any other time of day—which is true of life in general and especially true in camp. Even if you're a late sleeper, try to haul yourself out of the bag early. Morning events I keenly anticipate include watching the soft light grow slowly bright, gathering twigs and setting a small fire ablaze against a chill, peering into the forest in hopes of spotting nocturnal animals looking for a final snack before they seek their beds, listening to daybreak birdsong, splashing ice cold water on my face, and filling my lungs with cool fresh air delicately seasoned with pine sap and wild bloom. If things go perfectly, I have my first cup of coffee sitting quietly, alone or with my wife, before anybody else crawls out of a tent.

TIP

GENERAL CAMPING TIPS AND REMINDERS:

- During breakfast, the sleeping bags can be set out to air and dry.
- Don't leave camp for hiking, biking, or paddling before the bags are back in the tent, the tent is zipped shut, and the kitchen gear is stored.
- Store your food in a vehicle or in a cooler, and, if the cooler doesn't latch, place something heavy on top of it to keep feathered or furry camp raiders from getting in. Always leave the cooler in a shady spot.
- If you're leaving camp, the fire must be out, and the fire area tidied up.
- Leave the campsite tidied up. No one likes to come "home" to a messy camp, and neighbors won't like camping near someone else's messy camp.
- If you're leaving camp, and if you've befriended your neighbors, tell them you're off for a few hours or for the day and ask them politely to keep an eye on your site if they're staying put.
- If you're staying put, tidy up anyway. A tidy camp is a happier camp.

- In camp or on the trail, keep lunch simple, and keep it cold. There's too much to do, and it's too much bother, to cook and wash dishes and pots three times a day.
- Get ready for bed before dark. While plenty of sunlight is still shining down, check the tent. You can sweep out the dirt and debris you missed earlier, arrange the sleeping pads, fluff up the bags, and find the pillows.
- Before settling down around the fire with hot chocolate and marshmallows impaled on sticks, tidy up camp again. Store the food, put the cooler in your vehicle, put away those small items that might be lost in the bustle of the next morning, tighten the tent in case of rain, pick up the food scraps that will tempt animals into camp, and then relax. It has been a wonderful day, and now you're ready to have a wonderful evening.

Breaking Camp

Breaking down and packing up camp is a ritual for some, a haphazard affair for others. The best plan is to have a plan. The order in which camp is broken doesn't matter much—as long as everything is done and done well. You might, for example, leave the kitchen set up until last if you want a hot meal before hitting the road, or you might save the tent for last if you're considering a quick nap before a long drive.

1. *Leave the personal gear and clothing handy until the last minutes,* in case you want a quick tooth brushing or a clean shirt or pair of socks. Speaking of clean shirts, save one for the drive—almost everyone will appreciate it.
2. *Leave a trash bag out for the final bits of food and paper you pick up.* You can drop the trash bag in a camp receptacle on the way out or take it home to your garbage can.
3. *Let the tent dry as much as possible before packing it.* After the exterior of the tent's fly dries, remove it and drape it over a bush or tree limb with the interior exposed. After the tent dries, turn it bottom up and wipe off the pine needles and dirt. If dirt sticks tenaciously to the tent's bottom, wipe it clean with a damp paper towel—then let it rest bottom up to dry. If you have to pack the tent damp, you'll have to continue the drying at home (see Chapter 11). Wipe off the tent stakes, packing them clean and ready for the next trip.
4. *Give the sleeping bags time to dry before stuffing them into their bags.* Even if they feel dry, a half hour of hanging time will air them out, removing hidden moisture.
5. *Wipe off the stove and clean the kitchen gear before packing them.*

The Last Minute

With the vehicle packed, you're still not quite ready to drive away. Take a long, slow walk around your campsite with an eye peeled for the pocketknife half hidden by

Packing up to head home

leaves, the tent stake still stuck in the ground, and the little bits of food and trash overlooked as you cleaned the campsite. The next campers to use the site should find it in better condition than you did. You'll feel better, they'll feel better, and the world will be a tiny bit better place.

5

FAMILY MATTERS

If you have doubts, doubt no more: going camping with your family is good—from grandparents to great-grandchildren, it's good! It's a time that crams everything important about the physical aspects of being—food, shelter, warmth—into a small and lively space. It's a time of bonding and renewal, of growth as individuals and as a unit. If you pay attention, it's not only about seeing—people, places, the environment—but also about understanding. It's all about life—and it matters.

{ In the Words of a Sage }

Now I see the secret of making the best persons. It is to grow in the open air and to eat and sleep with the earth.

—Walt Whitman

The Children

Yes, one of the best things you can do for your kids is take them camping. They'll be stimulated physically, mentally, and emotionally. They'll grow stronger, learn great stuff, and maybe even enjoy the whole experience. But children are not small adults. They run differently, and they break down differently. Wise parents prepare appropriately and camp equipped with the know-how needed to care for their children outdoors.

Camping can be all about family.

Just the Facts: General Expectations by Age

Age	Expectations
0 to 6 months	Need constant attention, probably too young for camping.
6 to 12 months	Need almost constant attention, can ride in child carrier on a parent's back (as soon as child can hold his head up).
1 to 2 years	Need safe play area (playpen, padded tent floor), easy to entertain, need constant watching once they can toddle.
2 to 4 years	Very curious, might wander off, can carry light loads and pick up trash, can often walk a mile or more under their own power.
5 to 7 years	Still curious, still might wander off, can help with more involved camp chores (carrying water, unstuffing sleeping bags), may walk 2 to 4 miles under their own power at a slow pace.
8 to 9 years	Can be involved in almost all camp chores, can learn to read a map, can carry up to 20 percent of body weight in a pack, can often walk 5 to 7 miles at an easy pace.
10 to 12 years	Same as 8 to 9 years but can walk 8 to 10 miles at a moderate pace.
Teens	Same as 8 to 9 years but can do all camp chores as needed and walk up to 12 miles at an adult pace.

How Young Is Too Young?

The question perhaps should be this: when are the lives of babies enhanced by a camping experience? A child experiences immediate and immeasurable value from exposure to the mysteries and wonders of the natural world. Doctors generally suggest, however, that you wait until the child is five to six months old, with an established routine, and able to sit up without support.

Kids and Heat

Children get too hot faster than adults. The younger the child, the less developed the internal heat-regulating system.

- *Allow your children time to acclimatize to heat.* It will take them longer than it will take you. Early in the hot season, or early into a trip to an area hotter than your child is used to, go easy at first and increase the activity level progressively. The human body becomes increasingly able to adjust to heat.
- *Summer clothes should be constructed of cloth woven loosely* to allow air to circulate freely over the skin and moisture to evaporate freely off the skin. Snug-fitting clothing restricts healthy blood circulation and should be avoided. Wearing a hat, especially one with a wide brim, shades the heat-conscious brain and the sun-sensitive face.
- *Save strenuous exercise for the coolest times of the day*—early and late.
- *Encourage children to drink plenty of water* (see the following section).
- *Know how to treat overheated children.* They need rest in the shade and lots of fluids to drink, especially water. Loosen any restrictive clothing. Sponge or splash them with water and fan them to speed up the cooling.

Kids and Dehydration

Children need lots of water and dehydrate faster than adults, and excessive fluid loss can be devastating. One of the best and earliest signs of dehydration is urine color: clear indicates a well-hydrated child (or adult) and dark yellow indicates poor hydration. As dehydration grows worse, watch for headache, unusual fatigue, loss of appetite, nausea, and other complaints that make you think "flu." One of the later signs of serious dehydration in a child is restlessness and unusual loss of interest in whatever's going on around them.

KEEPING KIDS HYDRATED: Don't be surprised if kids say they don't feel thirsty. It's common for them to feel less thirst than do adults, but they still need to hydrate. If you find it difficult to get kids to drink plain water, add enough powdered flavoring to give the water some flavor but not enough to make it overly sweet.

TIP

Playing is good—but playing safe is better.

Kids and Sunshine

Children sunburn more easily than do adults, so they should wear clothing that is woven tightly enough to protect the skin from ultraviolet (UV) light. A hat with a brim to protect kids' faces is useful, as is sunscreen on unprotected skin. The sunscreen should be at least SPF 15, and some experts recommend SPF 30. Even though the damage may not show up for thirty years, 80 percent of skin damage from the sun (including skin cancers) happens in the first couple of decades of life.

SUN PROTECTION:

1. Do not use sunscreen on infants 0 to 6 months old. Their skin is too sensitive.
2. Keep children 0 to 12 months old out of direct sunlight as much as possible.
3. Test the sunscreen first on a small portion of skin, about the size of your hand, to see if the child will have a reaction. If the skin develops a rash, try a different brand.
4. Apply sunscreens in a uniform coat over all exposed areas.
5. If your trip involves swimming, use a waterproof sunscreen and reapply it often. A few inches of water will not protect your child's skin from sunburn.
6. Keep using the sunscreen even after a pleasant suntan is established. Tans prevent burning but offer little protection from the harmful effects of the sun.

7. Avoid the upper and lower eyelids where the sunscreen might be rubbed unintentionally into the eye.
8. Encourage children to wear sunglasses to reduce the chance of cataracts later in life and to protect their sensitive eyelids.
9. Never use baby oil in the sun.
10. If your child gets sunburned, start treatment as soon as possible. Cool, wet compresses may reduce the pain and limit the depth of the burn. Acetaminophen may be given for pain. Drinking lots of water is important in the treatment of sunburn.

Kids and Insects

Usually children have more trouble than adults resisting the temptation to scratch itchy bites. Because children typically pay less attention to hygiene and get dirtier than adults do, scratches on children have a higher rate of infection. Sting wipes may be used immediately to reduce the temptation to scratch. Hydrocortisone cream will reduce the itch of more established bites. Bites that are scratched open should be washed with soap and water and covered with a small adhesive strip.

INSECT REPELLENTS: Use DEET at a 30 percent or lower concentration. Or use a repellent that utilizes lemon eucalyptus oil: it works, it's the safest, and it smells better than DEET. Keep all repellent off kids' hands to reduce the likelihood that they'll rub it into their eyes or, even worse, suck it off their fingers.

TIP

Kids and Poisons

Small children make up the great majority of ingested-poison victims. In a suspected poisoning, you may consider inducing vomiting as soon as possible. First give the child water to drink—at least 8 ounces—then gently stimulate the gag reflex with your finger. Do *not* induce vomiting in children who (a) are having seizures, (b) are lethargic or in danger of further loss of consciousness, (c) have already vomited, (d) have ingested a corrosive substance (which usually produces burns on the lips or in the mouth), or (e) have ingested a petroleum product. If the child has ingested a poison, he or she should be evacuated to a medical facility as soon as possible, even if vomiting has occurred. Prevent poisoning by clearly identifying to the child anything in the environment that should be avoided and by keeping all dangerous substances out of reach.

MEDICATIONS FOR KIDS: Children aged five and under usually can't swallow pills, so carry children's medications in liquid form or chewable tablets. For children who don't yet chew, the tablets can be crushed and added to food. As with all medications, read the label carefully before use.

TIPS

KIDS AND OUCHIES: Little people get scraped and cut and blistered just like big people (see Chapter 8), but they sometimes make less-than-perfect patients. To encourage cooperation, carry kid-oriented wound management products for cuts and scrapes, such as adhesive strips, containers of anti-bacterial liquid soap, and premoistened towelette packages decorated with colorful characters.

FIRST-AID KIT FOR KIDS

In addition to your regular first-aid kit, carry the following for kid care:

- Foaming wound cleaner
- Colorful adhesive-strip bandages
- Liquid pain reliever
- Liquid antihistamine

SAFETY FIRST

The first steps at any campsite should be steps toward safety.

1. Keep the kids in sight at all times.
2. Older children can be assigned the responsibility of watching over younger children—but Grandma might prefer that job.
3. Walk the boundaries of your site with all the children, making sure they know exactly how far they can wander.
4. Point out obvious dangers to stay away from, such as a cliff or the bank of a river or lake.
5. Consider bringing a playpen for really small children.
6. If you see poisonous plants, point them out immediately to everyone.
7. Remind the kids to eat nothing—no berry, no leaf, no mushroom—unless Mom or Dad serves it to them.
8. Choose brightly colored clothing for your children. You'll be able to spot them more easily around camp—and on the trail during a hike.
9. Remind children of the importance of keeping *you* in sight at all times.

PADDLING PLAYPEN: If you've got a canoe, set it on the ground to serve as a temporary playpen for the really little ones.

CAMP CHORES: Camping is not a spectator sport. Almost everyone can be, and should be, given specific camp chores, such as these:

- Unpacking the vehicle.
- Setting up the tent.
- Spreading out the sleeping pads and bags in the tent.
- Preparing meals—or just helping.
- Cleaning up after meals.

- Picking up food scraps and trash.
- Gathering firewood.
- Putting out the fire.
- Hanging the sleeping bags to air.
- Stuffing the sleeping bags and rolling the pads.
- Gathering and packing personal items.
- Packing your vehicle.

OUTDOOR GEAR FOR KIDS: If you're interested, you can find excellent outdoor clothing and gear for kids (such as sleeping bags) in catalogs and on-line from companies such as Campmor *(www.campmor.com),* L. L. Bean *(www. llbean.com),* and REI *(www.rei.com).*

Keeping Kids Motivated

Attuned to the stimulation of electronics—TV, video games, movies—children often find the thought of camping "boring." They will be unmotivated, and you will have to produce the motivation. This is a challenge almost all parents

Everyone can help with camp chores.

face, but it's a challenge worth accepting. The rewards can be immediate (the children have a great time), and the rewards can be long-lasting (the children develop a deeper and fulfilling appreciation of the natural world). Nothing works every time, and sometimes you'll fail—but here are some proven suggestions:

- Create a sense of anticipation by describing the destination: a waterfall with a pool to wade in, a lake to swim in, a nature center, a nature trail.
- Read up on local flora, fauna, and history, and fill camp with interesting stories—for example, that acorns were roasted and pounded into flour to make a bitter bread eaten by Native Americans and early settlers, and that Benjamin Franklin wanted the wild turkey instead of the bald eagle as the symbol of the United States.
- Feed their curiosity. Take a close look at a caterpillar, an unusual flower, a colored rock, or fish swimming in the shallows of a creek. You don't have to know anything about natural history to foster wonder.
- Stay close to catch them, but let them climb rocks and trees if they want to—it's part of the fun of being a kid.
- Give a child a disposable camera and encourage the taking of pictures of what they want to remember.
- Carry treats as rewards for doing "this" or remembering "that."
- Share your enthusiasm. It can be contagious.
- Don't be disappointed if children lose interest quickly. It's part of being a child. There is always more to see and do.

Kids and Food

You want the kids to eat, and the kids need to eat, so make it better for everybody by packing foods you know the

Hiking can feed a child's curiosity.

kids enjoy. In fact, it's a great idea to talk over the menu with the kids before you go shopping. If they've had a say in what gets served, they're more likely to be interested in mealtime. You can also generate interest in mealtime by cooking creatively, such as stick cooking over the coals of a fire (see Chapter 7). *And remember:* snacks are good. Kids love snacks, and snacks work wonderfully to provide the tremendous energy kids will expend.

(see Chapter 7)

Good Eating: Snack Suggestions

Fruit, fresh and dried
Cheese sticks
Cookies
Candy
Banana bread
Muffins
Brownies
Pretzels
Crackers
GORP

DEFINING TERMS: *GORP* stands for "good old raisins and peanuts," a snack long favored by campers. But don't be limited by the name. You can add M&Ms, dried fruit, granola, yogurt-covered raisins or nuts or pretzels, chocolate chips, butterscotch chips—well, you get the idea.

TIP

Lost—and Alone

Whatever the chosen activity in or near camp, small children, despite being a source of delight, can become a source of anxiety. They can stray and, in the worst case, become completely lost.

- Teach your children what to do if they find themselves separated from you. They need to stay put, to "hug a tree," and to wait for you to find them. Tell them to respond if they hear anyone calling their name. This is an instance when a stranger might be a savior.

- Have your children carry some form of personal identification at all times. If someone else finds your lost child, identification will immediately tell them who the child is and, in most cases, that will reduce the amount of time you're separated. Identification can be as simple as a small card in a clothes pocket or as sophisticated as a Who's Shoes Kids ID Kit, a small strap with personal information that attaches to shoestrings with a Velcro closure.

Mama Kristin Speaks

Your best friends: baby wipes (for all ages), paper towels, and a supply of cotton bandannas. Store damp bandannas in zippered plastic bags so you'll have them on hand for wiping the peanut butter from their smiling faces. Wash and hang dry each night; reuse the next day!

INSTRUCTIONS FOR LOST KIDS: Write the following guidelines on an index card, and put the card in the small pack carried by children:

1. Stay put. Don't wander any farther.
2. Don't forget, I miss you and I'm looking for you.
3. Stay calm. Just sit down for a while.
4. Blow your whistle three times. That will tell me or someone else you need help.
5. Don't forget, I miss you and I'm looking for you.

WHEN LEAVING CAMP: If your children can carry a pack, even if it's only a very small pack, it's a great idea to get one for them. In addition to a favorite toy, give your child a small bottle of water or juice, a candy bar, and a whistle. Cut a hole in a plastic bag and stuff it in the bottom of the pack. A child can use the bag as a raincoat or an extra layer of clothing. Choose the brightest-colored garbage bag you can find in case you get separated from your child. Make sure the child knows *how* to use the whistle and the garbage bag.

PEER GROUP PRESSURE: At some point, kids will decide camping with grown-ups is "not fun." They develop a keen desire for the company of peers. Invite along one or more of your children's friends—and maybe an additional parent or two. It's a bit more work, but you'll love the results.

EDUCATIONAL MOMENTS: Explain everything you do, and why, in and around camp. Your "students" may not be eager, but the opportunity is too good to pass up. The rewards may not be immediately apparent—but the rewards are great.

The Elderly

Who is an "elderly" person? If you base your answer solely on chronology, most experts will tell you "old" starts at fifty-five—or at least you're "young old" at fifty-five. But if you're considering camping, it depends on other and more important factors, especially (a) how good your health is and (b) how well you are able to function outdoors. In other words, if your health and fitness don't preclude it, why not do it?

More and more members of the "gray group" are going camping—largely because they got hooked on camping when they were younger, and they still love doing it. That's not to say some older persons are not just beginning their camping lives. It can, however, be a tougher learning process for stiffer joints and muscles that ache with little abuse.

HOW OLD IS TOO OLD? Age is all in the mind: if you don't mind, it doesn't matter. In other words, if you're okay sleeping on the ground and sitting around a campfire, it's totally okay to do it.

Pre-Camping for the Elderly

If you're elderly and new to camping, or even if you're not so new to camping, you should have recently had a checkup done by your physician. Be sure you, and those going camping with you, know all about any conditions you may have, such as cardiovascular disease or hypertension. Let the physician know you're going camping, and tell her or him (a) the planned activities and (b) the anticipated environmental conditions—heat, cold, altitude, and so on. Ask for any specific guidelines or recommendations.

DISABLED CAMPERS: You'll find, with research, a growing number of campgrounds, pubic and private, with amenities—rest rooms and nature trails, for example—accessible to disabled persons. All public visitor centers are accessible.

It's a Dog's Life

Is Fido part of the family? If so, you may want to take the family pet camping with you. A dog will probably enjoy the experience as much as you do, romping around outdoors will be beneficial to your canine's health, and you won't have to find someone to dog-sit. Remember, though, that the dog, as a member of the camping party, will require as much and often more attention than at home.

The "Do's" of Dogs

- *Do make sure your dog's vaccinations are up to date.* There may be exposure to atypical germs, such as rabies. A call to the vet is a good idea.
- *Do have proper identification on your dog's collar.* Fluffy might get lost.
- *Do bring the dog's usual bowls and food*—and keep them available. Scavenging is an unhealthy act.
- *Do clean up after your dog.* Nobody wants to deal with the mess of someone else's dog.
- *Do think about where your dog will sleep:* a favorite sleeping pad, in the vehicle, in the tent?
- *Do make sure your dog is welcome in your chosen campground.* Dogs are not permitted in some campgrounds, such as most national parks, and sometimes you will be required to keep them on leashes. It is your responsibility to know and abide by the rules and regulations governing a dog in camp.

A dog is a furry member of the family.

The "Don'ts" of Dogs

- *Don't allow your dog to bother the neighbors.* It may seem like fun to you, but it may be a terrible irritation to your neighbors.
- *Don't allow your dog to chase wildlife.* It's bad for the wild animals, and it could be bad for your dog if the animal is a skunk, a porcupine, or some large and hungry critter. And it's probably illegal.
- *Don't assume your dog will be "fine."* It's a strange place with unpredictable dangers that you won't anticipate. Keep an eye on your pets, just like you keep an eye on your children.

Just the Facts: Is Your Dog a Welcome Guest?

Although specific regulations may vary, land management agencies, generally speaking, have these rules:

- National parks only allow dogs in campgrounds and on leashes.
- National forest campgrounds usually allow dogs.
- Bureau of Land Management campgrounds usually allow dogs.
- U.S. Fish & Wildlife Service campgrounds seldom allow dogs.
- State parks only allow dogs in campgrounds and on leashes, with a few exceptions.
- All campgrounds allow dogs assisting persons with disabilities, such as seeing-eye dogs.

CAMPFIRES

Something about a campfire, something indefinable that probably comes from way back in the firelit past, makes one infinitely appealing. A fire is heat for warmth and maybe for cooking. A fire is light. But it goes way beyond that, drawing people together, pulling an individual deeper inside her or his own mind and heart. More often that not, the campfire becomes the center of life in camp, especially in the evening. Most campgrounds will have a fire site ready for you. If not—and if fires are not banned—you'll have to prepare a fire site to have a fire (see Chapter 10). When you build a fire, whatever the reason or method, you must always undertake it responsibly.

{ In the Words of a Sage }

Having to squeeze the last drop of utility out of the land has the same desperate finality as having to chop up furniture to keep warm.

—Aldo Leopold

TECHNO: THE ELEMENTS OF FIRE

To build a fire, you need three basic ingredients: oxygen, heat, and fuel. Oxygen is waiting in the air. You'll apply heat with a firestarter, such as a match or lighter. You'll most likely have to gather the fuel, unless the campground offers it (a) pregathered and free or (b) pregathered and available for a fee.

Campfire Fuel

I divide campfire fuel into three categories: tinder, kindling, and fuel.

Tinder is any type of material that ignites with just a little heat—and the drier the tinder, the more easily it ignites. Dry grasses and dry pine needles make excellent tinder. Tiny twigs make great tinder, especially when they have tree resin in or on them. Even in very damp conditions, you often can find dry tinder beneath the low-hanging branches of dense evergreens and beneath trees that have toppled almost to the ground. You can also use paper, lint, charred cloth, steel wool, or firestarter blocks or tablets. All these materials ignite easily.

Kindling is the wood used to raise the heat from the burning tinder to a temperature that is high enough to ignite larger fuel. Larger dry twigs make excellent kindling. As for tinder, you can often find great kindling under coniferous trees where small, dead branches have fallen and been protected by the overhanging living tree. If the wood is about the diameter of a pencil and dry, it's probably good kindling.

Fuel usually consists of larger pieces of dry wood. For most uses, choose pieces no bigger that you can break with your hands. Large logs are part of a healthy ecosystem. If wood makes a sharp "snap" sound when you break it, it's plenty dry and ready to burn. Avoid rotted and crumbly wood, which might be dry but makes poor firewood and is well on its way to being naturally recycled into nutrition for living trees. *Gather firewood from the ground. Do not break or cut limbs from trees, dead or living.* Broken branches are unsightly and a scar on the tree and the forest.

TIP

GATHERING FIREWOOD: When you gather tinder, kindling, and fuel, collect at least twice as much as you think you'll need, especially tinder and kindling. If you fail at your first attempt at making a fire, you'll be glad you have more material close at hand. What you don't use can and should be scattered back into the environment, leaving no sign of your gathering.

Just the Facts: Why Dry Wood?

- Dry firewood ignites quicker.
- Dry firewood creates less smoke and a more pleasant fire for you and your neighbors.
- Dry firewood burns hotter and more completely, leaving less of a mess to clean up.

How to Make a Fire

1. With tinder, kindling, and fuel gathered, you are almost—but not quite—ready to apply the heat. The proper preparation of tinder is one of the most

critical factors in fire construction. Tinder must be arranged to allow air to flow around it. Fluff it up, if it fluffs, and stack it up loosely into the shape of a small volcano.

2. Over the bed of tinder, stack a small pyramid of kindling. The pieces of kindling should be close enough together for heat to jump easily from one piece to another. Don't stack kindling together tightly. Air must be able to flow around the material. Now it's time to apply heat to the tinder with a match or lighter or other form of firestarter.

3. Once your fire is going—the tinder gone, the kindling fully ablaze—you can start to add larger and larger pieces of fuel until the fire reaches the size you want. As you add fuel, place the pieces in a crisscross fashion to allow air to flow between them. You can smother a fire to death by piling on too much fuel.

BRING YOUR OWN FUEL: Some areas are notoriously devoid of firewood. To play it safe, many savvy campers gather tinder, kindling, and fuel prior to leaving home and carry it all with them in a box or bin.

TIP

TECHNO: BURN ONLY WOOD

Only wood and wood products (paper) will burn. Plastic will not burn, foil will not burn, glass will not burn, tin will not burn, and those materials should never go into a fire.

The Fire's End

Starting a fire is only half, or maybe less than half, the job. Ending the fire is usually a more critical undertaking.

- Stop adding fuel in time for the fire to die down in the evening.
- Push the unburned ends of fuel into the hot coals so they too will burn.
- When all the wood has burned to coals and ash, spread out the hot coals and toss on enough water or shovel on enough dirt to kill the fire before you go to bed.
- Before leaving camp for the day, check twice to make sure no heat remains in the fire.
- Before breaking camp, dig through the dead fire and remove any unburned trash.

- If the fireplace is full of ash and unburned pieces of wood, shovel all of it into a garbage bag and dispose of the bag in the campground's trash bin. Leave the fire site neat and ready for the next camper.

7

MEALTIME IN CAMP

Mealtime outdoors is special. Camp food seasoned with fresh air, consumed with appetites honed by exercise, is part of it. Meals you've eaten dozens of times may taste better than ever in camp. But more than that, camp meals are events: even if the group is not related by blood, the family comes together perhaps around the campfire, and the day either begins or is drawing to a close, and the mood is one of anticipation or recounting. It's a time of fortifying the body and of fortifying the spirit. It doesn't matter—much—what you eat: hot pancakes and maple syrup, peanut butter and jelly sandwiches washed down with orange juice, beef stew and savory biscuits. But you will want to plan well for mealtime. You'll find suggestions about planning and preparation in this chapter, as well as a handful of recipes.

{ **In the Words of a Sage** }

Prior planning prevents poor performance.

—Anonymous

Mealtime Planning

A couple of lists, separate and distinct from a general camping checklist, will help you to take good care of hungry campers.

You'll want a *menu list* based on the number of meals you'll eat and including what you plan to eat at each meal. Plan the order to your meals, too, using the items that might spoil before the less perishable items. You can create meals as simple or as complex as you wish. Plan on meals you know you enjoy, but be

Camp meals are not just about eating—they're an event.

ready to experiment, trying foods and recipes not typically found in your daily routine. That's part of the fun.

Remember to make a *food list* of the provisions you'll need to prepare each meal.

Good Eating: Sample Mealtime Plan

Day 1	Food needed
Breakfast	
Toast	Bread, butter, one dozen eggs,
Eggs	salt, pepper, bacon, coffee,
Bacon	orange juice
Coffee	
Orange juice	
Lunch	
Peanut butter/jelly sandwiches	Bread, peanut butter, jelly,
Potato chips	potato chips, Gatorade,
Gatorade	4 candy bars
Candy bars	
Dinner	
Spaghetti	Noodles, ground beef, one jar of
Rolls	sauce, rolls, lettuce, 2 tomatoes,
Salad	olives, 1 green pepper, 1 cucumber,
Wine	1 avocado, bottle of wine, cookies
Cookies	

Camp Stove Cooking

Camp stove cooking is, well, trickier that cooking at home. Start strong by giving yourself plenty of time to fix a meal. Until you have an understanding of camp cooking, give yourself twice the amount of time you think it would take you at home. For example, with almost all camp stoves it will take longer for water to reach the boiling point than on conventional stoves.

One of the worst things you can do at dinnertime is cook in the dark. The light of a lantern has many plusses, such as bringing people together in its warm glow, but preparing food is not one of them. You want to cook by natural light. Cleaning up after dinner is far easier in natural light, too, and that doesn't necessarily mean an early dinner since the sun sets late in summer, the season when most campsites are filled with folks like you.

Mama Kristin Speaks

Looking for a quick and easy breakfast that's sure to please even the fussiest eaters? Buy a variety pack of breakfast cereal in those single-serving cardboard boxes. Kids love cutting them open, peeling back the sides, adding milk, and eating right from the box.

TECHNO: GETTING THE MOST OUT OF CAMP STOVES

1. Get everything organized—the food, the utensils, the pots and pans—before you fire up the stove.
2. If your stove has more than one burner, the burner closest to the fuel source will produce the hottest flame. Start water boiling, and food cooking, on that burner, and if a second pot is required, move the first pot to the second burner for prolonged cooking time.
3. If food in one pot is ready to eat before you're ready to serve, cover it and set it near the stove or near the campfire to keep it warm while you finish cooking the remainder of the meal.
4. The pressure under which the fuel arrives at the burner can (and will) change over time. The fuel valves can become clogged with fuel residue, and the pressure in the tank can drop, requiring additional pumping. For those reasons, don't leave the stove unattended.

Camp Stove Recipes

This section is a camping cookbook of sorts. It in no way pretends to be exhaustive. It's just a collection of ideas in case your imagination needs some stimulation. The main point is this: you can enjoy awesomely good food with a little forethought and

Good Eating: Cook at Home

You can prepare complex (or simple) meals at home, freeze them in zip-top plastic bags, and simply warm them up at mealtime, using them as ice in your cooler until you want to eat them.

preparation and with little time spent laboring over a camp stove.

Breakfasts

An old adage strongly suggests that "Breakfast is the most important meal of the day." This is especially true when you're looking forward to a physically active schedule. You can get by with hot cereal or cold granola, but fire up the stove for a mouth-watering experience. And don't forget to start the coffee early (see "Cowboy Coffee").

Pancakes

Use a commercially available package of pancake mix, or work from scratch.

4 cups all-purpose flour (or substitute a cup of cornmeal or whole wheat flour for variety)
3 tablespoons baking powder
1 cup instant nonfat milk
¼ teaspoon salt

Mix these dry ingredients at home, and carry them in an airtight container. At mealtime, for about 8 to 12 pancakes, depending on their size, combine the following:

1¼ cup dry mix
1 egg
¾ cup water
1 tablespoon melted butter

Drop a glob of the batter onto a hot, greased frying pan or griddle. Fry until bubbles arise in the cake, then flip it and brown the other side. Serve with syrup, honey, brown sugar, jam, or another favored topping. You will receive a few more kudos by adding to the batter some fresh fruit, such as sliced bananas or strawberries, or a few nuts. You can even throw in a few chocolate chips to charm the kids and the kid in you. People who claim not to like pancakes have wolfed down a stack of these.

Daybreak Sandwiches

Bagel
Egg
Cheese
Ham, bacon, or sausage

If you're using ham or sausage, slice it thin. Fry the meat. Slice the bagel in half, butter each side generously, and heat it on a hot frying pan or griddle while an egg fries beside it. Flip the bagel and add a slice of cheese, allowing it to soften a bit. Put it all together for an utterly delicious sandwich. This recipe only makes one, but be prepared to make a lot more.

Good Eating: Cowboy Coffee

No coffeepot? Don't despair. All you need is an old pot and lots of ground coffee beans. For every cup of water in the pot, approximately, put in a heaping tablespoon of coffee, approximately. Put the pot on the stove and watch it impatiently. You don't want it to boil and grow bitter. Just as the black water starts to move around, take the pot off the stove, cover it, and wait a few minutes for the grounds to settle. Pour off a steaming cup while unsuccessfully trying to keep all the grounds in the pot. Later you spit out the grounds that work their way into your mouth. This is a necessary and treasured aspect of cowboy coffee. If you choke a little on the first and last swallow, it's probably just right.

Entrées

Sure, hot dogs, hamburgers, and grilled chicken make great camp food, so include them in your menu. Add a bowl of potato salad you whipped up at home and kept chilled in the cooler. But consider a few other options.

Burritos

Tortillas
Ground beef, pork, or turkey
Tomato sauce
Chili powder
Cheese, grated
Refried beans, canned
Vegetables, fresh chopped (lettuce, tomatoes, peppers, onions, etc.)
Sour cream, guacamole, salsa (optional)

Cook the ground beef with the tomato sauce in a frying pan or saucepan, and season it to taste with chili powder. Warm the beans in a separate pot, or right in the can. Heat a tortilla for a minute or so in another hot frying pan. Have everybody roll his or her own burrito. All diners will be outrageously happy.

Smoked Salmon Pesto Pasta

8 ounces smoked salmon
8 ounces angel-hair pasta
2 ounces sun-dried tomatoes
1 tablespoon pesto (more if you're a pesto fan)
1 tablespoon olive oil
1 ounce pine nuts
Parmesan cheese, to taste

Toss the pasta into boiling water. A few minutes before the pasta reaches *al dente,* add the sun-dried tomatoes so they'll hydrate. With the pasta cooked to satisfaction, drain it, and add the salmon after breaking it into small chunks. Add the pesto, oil, and a generous sprinkling of pine nuts and parmesan, mixing well. (If you forgot the salmon, this still tastes great.) Serves 4.

Spicy Fried Fish

About 8 ounces filleted fish
4 tablespoons vegetable oil
¼ cup melted butter
Red pepper
Lemon wedges

Heat the oil in a frying pan until it just about smokes. While the oil heats up, coat the fish in melted butter and rub in enough pepper to suit your taste. Cook the fish in the hot oil for 1 to 3 minutes, depending on the thickness of the fillets. The fish will be lightly blackened on both sides when done. (*Note:* firm fish, such as halibut, works great, but soft fish, such as trout and catfish, also work well if you turn the fillets carefully.) Squeeze on a splash of lemon juice and serve.

Spanish Rice

2 cups water
1 cup instant rice
1 to 2 tablespoons onion flakes
½ cup chopped red and green bell pepper
1 cup dried tomatoes
2 cups instant tomato soup
2 cups water
1 bouillon cube
1 tablespoon cooking oil
½ teaspoon garlic powder
½ teaspoon basil

½ teaspoon oregano
½ teaspoon chili powder
1 cup grated cheese
Black pepper and cayenne, to taste

Bring water to a boil. Add bouillon cube, then stir in the rice, onion flakes, chopped peppers, tomatoes, and instant soup. Simmer for 5 minutes. Remove from heat and let stand covered for 5 minutes more. Place the oil in a frying pan. Add the rice mixture and all the remaining spices. Fry to desired crispiness, top with cheese, cover, and set aside to allow cheese to melt. Serves 2–3.

Desserts

Everyone loves dessert. It can be a bag of store-bought cookies—or it can be a memorable treat without much work.

Triple-Threat Chocolate Pudding

8 chocolate sandwich cookies
1 tablespoon chocolate sprinkles
1 package instant chocolate pudding
1 cup instant nonfat milk powder
1 cup cold water

Place the cookies in a zip-top plastic bag and crush them thoroughly by squeezing with your hands. Add the sprinkles, pudding mix, and milk powder to the bag, and mix well. (You can do all that at home.) In camp, add the water to the bag and shake it like crazy for about 3 minutes. Place it in the cooler until the pudding solidifies. You'll probably wish you had doubled the recipe.

No-Bake Cookies

½ cup water
½ cup margarine
2 tablespoons instant nonfat milk powder
2 cups sugar
3 tablespoons cocoa powder
3 cups quick-cooking oats
½ cup peanut butter
1 cup chopped nuts (optional)

Mix the water, margarine, milk, sugar, and cocoa powder in a pot, and bring the mixture to a boil. Remove from the heat and immediately mix in the remaining ingredients. Press into the bottom of a pan, cover, and set aside to cool. Cut and serve.

Peanut Butter Pie

¼ cup margarine
¾ cup crunchy peanut butter
3¼ cups (½ pound) powdered sugar
¾ cup graham cracker or cookie crumbs
1½ cups chocolate chips

Melt the margarine and mix in the peanut butter, sugar, and crumbs. Press the mixture into the bottom of a round pan (so it looks like a pie). Melt the chips and pour them over the top. Chill for and hour or so, if you can wait that long.

Campfire Cooking

Not so very long ago everything was cooked over the coals or, sometimes, over the flames of an open fire. That's rapidly becoming a lost art. Camping gives you the opportunity to rekindle the art—and you just might want to give it a try. You might not like it, but you just might like it a lot.

If the fireplace has a grate, and campground fireplaces often do, you may be set to go—but you may not. The fireplace may look like half a barrel buried in the ground and topped with several thick iron bars. First, you can't grill meat on the thick iron bars because they won't transmit enough heat. Second, it's difficult to maintain decent cooking coals in such a fireplace because you get little of the necessary circulation of air to the coals. However, you may be able to flip the iron bars out of the way so you can place your own grill nearer the coals, and then you'll be set.

You're usually better off purchasing an inexpensive, collapsible grill that either stands on legs of its own or rests on two logs or rocks set across from each other. A grill 20 to 24 inches long and about the same width will work fine.

Cooking without a grate or grill is a tedious affair, often resulting in a ruined meal. In fact, it is impossible to grill meat without a grate or grill. Thus, this method is not highly recommended (see "Cooking Fires").

TECHNO: COOKING FIRES

1. Keep your cooking fire small. You don't need an awful lot of heat, and the heat you make must be concentrated under the pot, pan, or meat sizzling on the grill. Most campfire meals are actually cooked over coals since flames create far too much heat.
2. Gather enough firewood to avoid a trip for more in the middle of meal preparation.
3. Remember that a pot will get very hot over the coals of a fire. You'll need durable gloves, padded kitchen mitts, and/or potgrips to safely lift a pot from the heat.

If you haven't tried cooking on a fire, your camping life is missing something.

GARBAGE CAN (LID) GRILLING: Consider carrying an old metal garbage can lid, shoveling hot coals into the lid, and using your own grill over the coals in the lid.

TECHNO: **COOKING ON COALS**

- The biggest mistake made in campfire cooking is not building the fire soon enough to allow it time to burn down to coals.
- When the wood has burned down to coals a couple of inches thick, you're usually ready to cook.
- If you can hold your hand six to eight inches over the coals for six to eight seconds, the temperature is just right.
- Check the coals now and then as the food cooks, and add more *small* pieces of wood if the temperature drops too much.
- You can scrape coals off to the side of a big fire for cooking, but make sure they are far enough away to prevent too much heat from reaching the pot or pan during meal preparation.
- Don't forget that food cooking over a fire, small or large, should never be left alone. Fire can turn what would have been a tasty meal into a charred ruin in a very short time.

HEATING WATER:

- Water will boil faster when it's suspended over flames instead of over hot coals.
- You can hang a pot with a handle from a stick buried deep in the ground and tilted over the flames.
- You can place a pot on a grate over flames.

Grilling Meat

Set the grill about six to eight inches above the coals to grill meat. If the coals are too hot, you can prop the grill higher. If the coals are not hot enough, build up the coals before grilling.

Just the Facts: How Much Heat for the Meat?

How long you cook meat depends on many variables, such as the amount of heat and the thickness of the meat. The primary variable is how well you like your meat cooked:

Rare—pink and cool in the center.
Medium rare—pink and warm in the center.
Medium—brown in the middle.
Well done—sort of like leather but easier to eat, sometimes.

You can make small slices in the meat now and then to check the color, but in all cases take the meat off the grill sooner rather than later. You can always cook it more, but you can't un-cook it.

{ Personal Reflections }

I like my meat medium rare. I grill one side for a couple of minutes, and then flip the meat. After a couple more minutes, I press on the meat with my finger. If it's really soft, I let it grill a bit more. When it's starting to feel firm, it's usually just right for me.

Shish Kebabs

1 pound of steak, lean and expensive
1 large, firm tomato
1 green bell pepper
1 large, sweet onion
6 mushrooms
Teriyaki sauce

You'll also need four or five skewers. You can whittle skewers from wood or carry metal ones. (To prevent the skewers from burning, soak them in water prior to using them.) Cut the meat into chunks and let it marinade in teriyaki sauce for an hour or so in the cooler. Cut the vegetables into golf-ball-size chunks. Thread the meat and vegetables onto separate skewers. The veggies will cook faster, and you don't want burned onions sitting next to raw meat. Leave a tiny bit of space between each skewered chunk. Place the skewers on the grill, basting them with fresh teriyaki sauce each time you turn them. As dinner cooks, you can explain to fascinated watchers that *shish kebab* comes from the Turkish word for this form of cooking. Check often, and remove the skewers when the meat is cooked to your satisfaction. A pound of steak should feed four people.

Grilling Corn on the Cob

Any meat, for that matter just about any campfire meal, finds a great companion in grilled corn on the cob. Don't remove the husks! Simply slice off the stem and the small end, and soak the whole thing in water for a few minutes. Place them on the grill well before you start the meat cooking. The husk may blacken alarmingly, but the corn inside is what counts. Peel back the husk now and then to check on the tenderness of the corn.

If you prefer, peel the husk back but not off. Smother the corn on the cob in butter and garlic powder, and push the husk back in place. Wrap each ear in foil and cook them all on the grill.

CHARCOAL BRIQUETTES: You don't have to, and may not be able to, depend on natural sources of coals. If you want to be sure of having enough hot coals, pack a bag of charcoal briquettes. You can use them alone or with natural sources of heat.

Cooking with Pots and Pans

Cooking with pots and pans over a fire differs from stovetop cooking only in how you manage the heat. To lower the heat, you can move the pot off to the side of the fire or raise it higher above the fire. You can throw a few more sticks on the coals to raise the heat.

You will need a proper pot. A proper pot has a snug-fitting lid. Without the lid, the food soon acquires a distinctive smoky taste, which is fine with a hot dog but disgusting in oatmeal or spaghetti. A snug lid also means your water will boil faster.

If you plan to use a frying pan, choose one with a long handle to make life easier. Otherwise, cooking with a pan differs only, as you now know, in how you manage the heat.

Flip-Baked Bread

2 cups flour
¼ cup dry milk
4 teaspoons baking powder
Pinch of salt
1¼ to 1½ cups water
¼ cup cooking oil

Mix the dry ingredients well. Slowly add the water, mixing it in until your dough has the consistency of thick mud. It should slide off your spoon, but it shouldn't be in a hurry. Smear your frying pan well with cooking oil. (You can use butter, but you have to be very careful not to let your pan get too hot.) Press the dough gently into the pan, and place the pan over hot coals. When the edges get sort of brown, flip the dough over carefully and continue cooking until both sides are toasty and the middle is not gooey. The time per side depends on the thickness of the dough and the heat of the fire. When the bread is done, it will have a hollow sound when you thump it with a flicked finger. You can vary this recipe by substituting a cup of cornmeal for a cup of flour and end up with flip-baked cornbread. Or you can throw ½ cup of sugar into the dry ingredients, maybe a handful of raisins, and end up with a sweet bread.

Frypan Oat Cakes

½ cup cooking oil
½ cup sugar
2 tablespoons dry milk
About 1 cup water
2¼ cups white flour
1 cup wheat flour
¾ cup oatmeal
1 teaspoon salt
2 teaspoons baking powder
1 teaspoon cinnamon

Mix the oil, sugar, dry milk, and water in a pot and bring the mixture to a boil. Stir until the sugar is dissolved and remove it from the heat. Add the rest of the dry ingredients to the sugary milk mixture, and stir until all ingredients are moist. You'll now have dough from which you can pinch off balls that you shape into round cakes. Press the round cakes gently into a well-greased frying pan and flip-bake as described in the recipe for Flip-Baked Bread. Make more than you can eat. They'll last quite a while in your pack on a day hike.

BLACKENED CAMPFIRE GEAR: Fires will blacken pots, pans, and grills considerably. That's okay. Think of the black like a karate master's belt. It shows you've put in your time beside a cooking fire. But keep a large plastic bag handy to carry the blackened gear. That way your vehicle and other stuff will stay unblackened.

Cooking with a Dutch Oven

A Dutch oven is the most versatile apparatus ever made for cooking on a fire. It was the only cooking gear carried by the Corps of Discovery, otherwise known as the Lewis and Clark Expedition. Despite the name, the Dutch oven is an American invention, and credit goes to the Pennsylvania Dutch. Inside a Dutch oven you can shallow fry, deep fry, roast, bake, poach, or stew, as well as boil. You can turn the lid inside out and use it as a griddle to fry, say, eggs and bacon. A well-made Dutch oven has a strong handle for easier lifting. Made of cast iron, a Dutch oven tends to be heavy, and even more so with food in it, so take care when lifting a full one from the fireplace.

One problem of Dutch oven cooking over wood coals is that such coals sometimes lose their heat before the food is cooked. For that reason, it works best to scrape hot coals off toward the side of the fire. When the coals under, or over, the oven die, you can add more coals from those you've set aside. Remember that the heat from a nearby fire will also add heat to the oven, so turn the oven occasionally to distribute the heat more evenly as the food cooks.

Almost any recipe will work in a Dutch oven. Use an oven as you would a pot or frying pan for boiling or frying. If you're going to roast, bake, or stew, place the Dutch oven directly in the coals, bank the coals around the oven, and pile more coals on top of the oven, being sure to seat the lid well first. You'll need quite a few coals, and those on top will particularly need replacing from time to time to keep enough heat on all sides of the baking food. You can, for example, pack in a box of commercially prepared cake mix and bake up a sumptuous dessert in a Dutch oven. If you're following a recipe, a Dutch oven typically requires approximately the same amount of time to roast, bake, or stew as your home oven does, if you keep the coals appropriately hot.

TECHNO: DUTCH OVENS AND BRIQUETTES

Because wood coals lose heat a lot faster than charcoal briquettes, many modern Dutch oven chefs prefer briquettes. This is a great idea—with one potential problem: novice cooks often fail to realize just how much heat is released by briquettes. For

Continued

high heat, you need only one layer of briquettes under the kettle. For medium heat, which is a good baking temperature, you need only a layer of briquettes spread apart approximately the width of each briquette under the kettle. Baking will also require a layer of briquettes, spread out on the lid about a briquette's width apart. You can add or subtract, of course, to adjust the heat, just as you add or subtract wood coals (and a camp shovel comes in mighty handy). It takes a little experimentation, but for the Dutch oven enthusiast, it's wonderful fun.

TIP

CAST-IRON CARE: Because a Dutch oven is made of cast iron, it requires special care. Before use it must be "seasoned." Wash it at home with warm soapy water, dry it thoroughly, and, using a paper towel, wipe a coat of vegetable oil over the entire surface, inside and out, including the lid. In your oven at home, bake the kettle and lid, lid ajar, at 250 degrees for about an hour and a half. The "seasoning" is now complete. From now on *never* wash your Dutch oven with soap. After use, scrape out the food scraps and scrub the oven clean with just a little water. Then wipe on a light coat of fresh oil. Over time, the surface will acquire a dark and shiny look, and that's good. Every time you use it, wipe on a little fresh vegetable oil and preheat the Dutch oven to ready the seasoning. In storage, don't set the lid tightly in place. Ventilation will prevent the oil coating from becoming rancid.

Dutch Oven Pork Chops

4 or 5 pork chops
Potatoes, sliced (about one per person)
1 medium onion
1 can of cream of mushroom soup with half the water called for on the can

Oil and preheat the Dutch oven. Brown the chops on both sides. Toss in the potatoes, then the onions. Pour the soup over everything. Bury the oven in hot coals. Check the contents periodically since cooking time will vary depending on the thickness of the chops and how well you maintain the heat. Dinner should be ready in about an hour.

Dutch Oven Biscuits

2 cups all-purpose flour
2 teaspoons baking powder
¼ teaspoon baking soda
1 teaspoon salt
¼ cup butter
¾ cup milk

Oil and preheat a Dutch oven. Mix the dry ingredients in a bowl, or—even better—premix them at home and carry them in a zip-top plastic bag. In a bowl, cut the butter into the mix with a knife until the butter chunks are no bigger than peas. Add the milk and stir ingredients together. Knead the dough briefly, and flatten it on a plate or cutting board. With a coffee mug, cut out the biscuits. Place the biscuits on the bottom of the prepared Dutch oven, allowing a tiny space between each biscuit. You want medium heat, so place about 1 inch of hot coals beneath the oven and 1.5 inches on top. When the biscuits are brown on the sides, remove the oven from the coals on the bottom but leave the coals on top until the tops of the biscuits brown.

Dutch Oven Rice

2 large onions
Bacon, several strips
Butter
2 cups hot water
1 cup quick-cooking rice
1 large tomato
Pinch of salt
Grated cheese

Chop the onions and bacon as the oiled Dutch oven heats in the coals. Stir-fry the onions and bacon (with a dab of butter for extra flavor) for a few minutes. Add 2 cups of hot water to the oven with the cup of rice—and for Pete's sake don't stir the rice. Place the lid securely on the oven. While the rice cooks, cut up the tomato. When the rice is cooked, remove the oven from the heat, mix with the tomato and salt, and sprinkle the grated cheese on top.

Dutch Oven Cobbler

3 cups fresh fruit (blueberries, blackberries, sliced apples, and such)
1 cup all-purpose flour
1 cup whole wheat flour
2 teaspoons baking powder
¼ teaspoon salt
½ cup butter
1 cup sugar
¾ cup milk
Whipped cream

Mix the flours, baking powder, and salt—or once again bring them mixed from home. Soften the butter and beat the butter and sugar in a bowl until the mixture is fluffy. Add the flour mixture and milk to the bowl and beat the mixture until it's smooth. Spread the smooth batter over the bottom of an oiled Dutch oven. Push up the side of the batter, as if you were crimping a pie. Place the fruit on top of the batter. About 45 minutes of baking later, with coals below and above, and you'll have dessert ready to serve with whipped cream on top.

Foil Cooking

Aluminum foil will not burn, and that can work in your favor if you choose the simple campfire cooking method of placing foil-wrapped food directly in coals. (Be careful, though, because aluminum foil can fall apart if exposed to too much heat.) Many foods (such as meat, potatoes, onions, carrots, squash, and apples) can be foil-cooked. Before placing the foil-wrapped food in the coals, let the coals die down more than you would when using other methods. Don't worry if the coals have turned a cold-looking grayish-white. White ash will hold the heat underneath for an adequate amount of time to make dinner in foil. With the food prepped, snuggle the foil-wrapped package deeply in the coals and enjoy another cup of coffee, tea, or hot chocolate while the grub cooks.

TIP

COOKING IN FOIL:
- Use heavy-duty foil.
- Tear off a piece large enough to allow you to tightly seal the food inside with at least a double fold at each end. Place the food on the foil, flatten the edges of the foil, and fold the edges over about three-quarters of an inch. Then fold the edge a second time, and maybe a third.
- You can prevent sticking, and improve flavor, by rubbing plenty of butter on the inside of the foil before adding the food.
- Onions are especially difficult to ruin. If the taste of onion will benefit the meal, a bottom layer of onions will enhance flavor, even if the onions burn.
- Don't leave the food in the heat any longer than necessary. The food may burn, and the foil will begin to fall apart.
- When you think the coals have done their job, fish out a package and press it with a gloved hand. If you've included vegetables, a nice squishy feel usually means the cooking has gone long enough. If you're cooking only meat, it will feel firm when pressed.
- If you unwrap the food and find it not yet cooked to your satisfaction, you can return it to the coals for more cooking.

Potato-in-Foil

1 large baking potato
1 large onion
Butter

Slice the potato almost all the way through in a half dozen or so places. Make sure you don't slice it through completely. Cut the onion into slices, and place a slice of onion in each cut in the potato. Fold the whole thing securely in butter-smeared foil. Place it in the coals for about 45 minutes. Enjoy some cheese and crackers, or conversation, or the sunset. When you think the potato is done, stick a fork through the foil. When the potato is done, the fork will slip out without lifting the potato. For a taste bonus, sprinkle on some grated cheese, or some salt and pepper, or both, after unwrapping the spud.

Hamburger-in-Foil

½ pound ground beef or turkey
1 carrot
1 small potato
1 small onion
Butter

Cut up the vegetables. Form the meat into a patty. Smear some butter on the foil, as always, and place some of the vegetables on the foil, then the patty, then the rest of the vegetables. Close the foil securely and snuggle the package into the coals. Cook about 12 minutes, roll over the foil package, and cook another 12 minutes. Take care when you turn over the package because you don't want to tear the foil. To save time, you can prepare this foil dinner before leaving home and carry it in a plastic bag in case juice leaks out. Don't be afraid to add other ingredients you like to the recipe, such as green pepper, tomato, and pineapple.

Stick Cooking

No campfire cooking method is simpler, in terms of utensils, than stick cooking—although you're somewhat limited in what you can cook with this method: meat, or vegetables cut small but not so small that they fall apart when you skewer the pieces, or some type of dough you can wrap around the stick (see the recipes that follow). Cooking on a stick promises to be a lot of fun—especially for the kids. You'll need a stick about a half inch thick and, say, four feet long—or, if you've planned ahead, carry a coat hanger with you to unbend into a "stick."

COOKING ON A STICK:

- A wooden stick should be sharpened on one end.
- If the bark is still on the stick, leave it on in most cases, but do wash the cooking end, rubbing off any loose bark and debris. A little bark can prevent food from rotating when you turn the stick over the coals, a situation that could leave you frustrated *and* with a half-cooked dinner.

TIPS

- Fish can be spitted through the mouth and into the intestinal cavity.
- Red meat should be cut no more than an inch thick and pulled onto the spit through pre-sliced holes.
- You can hold skewered food over the coals, if you're patient, or prop one end of the stick over a rock or log with the other end held down by a second rock or log.
- Slow cooking creates a tastier meal, so don't suspend the food too close to the coals. If you have too much heat, the outside of food chars while the inside stays raw.
- Rotate the stick when the surface of the food facing the heat appears done.
- With several variables at play, the best way to know when the food is cooked to your taste is by tasting it.

STICK COOKING ON METAL: If you've chosen to cook on a metal hanger or some other metal skewer, remember that the entire length of metal may grow hot before dinner is ready, so wear gloves to handle the metal.

Those who are deeply committed to stick cooking on a coat hanger can make a handle by splitting a short piece of wood, slipping one end of the hanger into the split, and tying the split wood closed securely around the hanger.

Stick Bread

1 cup all-purpose flour
1 teaspoon baking powder
Pinch of salt
1 or 2 tablespoons powdered milk (optional, for more protein)
1 tablespoon butter or cooking oil
A little water

Few campfire foods have as much appeal and offer as much satisfaction as fresh bread. This recipe is for the basic bannock (bread) of yesteryear, and it can be cooked when the nearest utensil is dozens of miles away. Don't mix the ingredients until you've prepared the fire and the stick. In fact, if you don't want to mix the ingredients at all, carry Bisquick. The stick you use should be peeled down to bare wood—no bark. Thoroughly mix the flour, baking powder, and salt (and

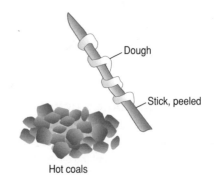

Cooking bread on a stick.

powdered milk if you choose to use it). Soften the butter near the heat, and then mix it well with the dry ingredients. Add just enough water to make a firm dough. With too much or too little water, the dough won't adhere to the stick, which it must. If the water is really cold, first warm it a bit by the fire. Warm water encourages the baking powder to do its job of fluffing up the dough when it cooks. *Hint:* it's easier to add a little more water than a little more flour to reach the right consistency, so add water slowly. When you can toss the dough ball easily from hand to hand, it's probably ready. Roll it out in your hand until it's long and slim, then wrap it around the stick and bake it over the coals. When it's golden brown on the outside, it's usually ready. For a dessert option, add dried fruit, sugar, cinnamon, and so on to the dry mix, then add water and bake.

S'Mores

The most famous stick-prepped snack of all time, s'mores, in case you didn't know, got their name from the claim that once you eat one you'll want "some more." The original s'more is made of graham crackers, milk chocolate, and marshmallows. Break the graham cracker in half and lay a chunk of chocolate on one half. Roast a marshmallow or two on a stick or coat hanger until you've got a mass of thoroughly hot sugar. Pull the marshmallow off the stick by placing it on the chocolate and pressing the second half of the cracker against it, then gently remove the stick. Give the resulting cookie a minute or two so the chocolate can melt. Don't be constrained by the original recipe. Use your imagination. A rice cake instead of a graham cracker, for example, yields a totally delicious snack—and it's bigger!

Spit Cooking

When you want to cook something large, something that doesn't skewer well when cut up in small pieces, such as a chicken or a small furry mammal (with fur removed), you'll do better by spit cooking, a glorified method of stick cooking. In this case, the skewered meat is held over the coals by propping up both ends of the stick. A popular method of suspension is to bury forked sticks in the ground on both sides of the fire, but you can also stack rocks on both sides of the fire and lay the spit across the top of the stacks. A spit allows you to easily rotate your dinner over the coals, and rotate you should every three or four minutes.

Be prepared for a long wait. Spit cooking takes a lot of time. You can speed up the process with an old mountain man technique. Slice off the outer layer of meat after it has cooked, and eat it while the next layer cooks. You never get the really tender inner meat that long, slow cooking produces, but you get to eat sooner.

SPIT COOKING:

- To skewer an animal on the spit, run a sharp stick from head to tail along the underside of the backbone. (To prevent the stick from burning, soak it in

TIP

water prior to using it.)

- Many woods will add an unpleasant taste to meat, but searing the stick in the heat of the fire first will eliminate most of the taste of wood.
- Searing the meat first will seal in the juices, making your repast less dry and more tasty.

If You Hate to Cook

If cooking has no appeal whatsoever, you do have some options other than the usual freeze-dried smorgasbord of products.

Meals, Ready-to-Eat (MRE)

Thank the United States military for these meals. In a full field package MRE, you will find entrée, bread, dessert, snack, juice, coffee, gum, and even a spoon and napkin, all packaged in indestructible plastic bags. You might see similar products, at least the entrées, on supermarket shelves being sold as "retort" foods—foods that have been cooked and sealed in a flexible foil package that you reheat in hot water. MREs are sometimes available in army–navy surplus stores, on the Internet, and occasionally in outdoor specialty stores.

Grocery Store and Go

You can walk out of your favorite food market with instant cereals, such as oatmeal and cream of wheat. Add some butter, nuts, and/or dried fruit to amplify the taste and up the nutrition. You can also purchase tea, instant coffee, sugar, and powdered milk for hot drinks and camp stove recipes. Instant soups are available by the ton, including the perennially favorite ramen noodles. Or pick up a few varieties of dinner-in-a-bag. They take about ten minutes of boiling, and usually require adding milk (instant works fine) and butter or margarine.

Cold Camping

No fire, no stove, no mess, no bother—and no hot food: these are the elements of cold camping. Break your fast with bagels and cream cheese or granola and reconstituted powdered milk. Add some dried fruit for flavor and a nutritional boost. Lunch on trail mix, fruit bars, energy bars, fresh fruit, meat sticks, cheese, crackers, pita bread, or more bagels. Dine on the same. Drink water, or add some rehydrated fruit-drink crystals or a powdered energy drink for variety and a few more calories.

8

CAMP FIRST AID

Bad things can happen when you're camping, but then bad things can happen at home, too. What you should be ready to do, in camp and at home, is to provide first aid in an emergency. This section is *not* a first-aid course. This is not even a first-aid manual. As mentioned previously in this book, the well-prepared camper has taken a first-aid course and carries a first-aid manual. What this chapter does is prepare you, if you've packed an adequate first-aid kit (first see Chapter 2), to handle the most common problems: the ones that show up now and then in camp.

{ **In the Words of a Sage** }

You'll break the worry habit the day you decide you can meet and master the worst that can happen to you.

—Arnold Glasow

911: Does the campground have access to 911 via a camp phone or your cell phone? Find out when you check in, and find out where you can access the nearest phone if you don't have a cell phone that will pick up a transmitting signal there. In an emergency, calling 911—if you can—is the next thing to do after checking that it is safe to approach the injured or ailing person.

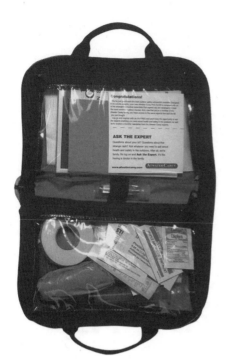

Bites and Stings

Most campers spend at least a little time worrying about the creatures that can bite or sting. Some of this worry is justified. Mosquitoes, for example, can swarm with enough ferocity to ruin an otherwise splendid campsite. Still, serious bites and stings are rare.

Small Insects

The little biters—mosquitoes, black flies, gnats, and such—tend to be the most bothersome but the least serious problem in terms of first aid. A wipe with a sting relief product can ease the itching after a bite. Antihistamines, especially diphenhydramine, can reduce itching and the swelling of more severe reactions.

You must be prepared to give first aid.

TIP

PREVENTING INSECT BITES:

- Wear clothing that insects cannot penetrate with their stingers, pincers, or jaws.
- Wear insect repellent on skin. Follow the directions on the label carefully with all products, especially with products containing DEET. If you prefer to go non-DEET, try products containing lemon eucalyptus oil.
- Treat clothing and tents with permethrin. Permethrin is actually a synthetic insecticide, and it is safe to use and effective against insects and ticks.

Bees and Their Relatives

The stinger left by honeybees should be removed as soon as possible. Despite thoughts to the contrary, any means to get it out is acceptable. Ice or cold packs on the stings from bees, wasps, yellow jackets, hornets, and fire ants will relieve pain and reduce swelling. Diphenhydramine may be effective in reducing itching and swelling.

Spiders

Two species of spiders are of concern:

Black widows are shiny with an hourglass shape almost always on the abdomen.

They have a bite that often goes unnoticed, but local pain and redness show up at the bite site within an hour. Severe pain from muscle cramping usually develops in the bitten arm or leg and in the abdomen and back. The pain may be incredibly severe. Fever, chills, sweating, and nausea may develop. Ice or cold packs applied to the bite site usually provide some relief. Pain-killing drugs may be used, if available. Although most of those bitten recover within twenty-four hours, evacuation to a doctor is strongly recommended, especially for children and the elderly.

Brown recluse (fiddleback) spiders have a violin shape on their backs and a bite that usually produces local pain and blister formation within a few hours. A discoloration shaped like a bull's-eye often surrounds the blister. The blister eventually ruptures and leaves a growing ulcer of dead tissue. Ice or cold packs can relieve local pain. Pain-killing drugs may be useful. If the blister ruptures, treat the open wound appropriately. Anyone who has been bitten by a brown recluse should be seen by a physician to minimize damage and to consider appropriate medicines.

Scorpions

Stings from scorpions produce immediate pain, soon followed by swelling. Sometimes the sting site becomes numb. Ice or cold packs will reduce pain. Diphenhydramine can reduce swelling and itching. Recovery is almost always rapid—except sometimes from the sting of *Centruroides*, a southwestern scorpion that may produce a systemic reaction characterized by unusual anxiety, sweating, salivation, gastrointestinal distress, and, most importantly, respiratory distress. No specific first aid is useful for *Centruroides* stings, and an immediate trip to a doctor should take place.

Ticks

The little eight-legged tick, in numerous species, may carry diseases that it can pass to humans. Insect repellents repel ticks, and ticks crawling around on your skin do not transmit diseases until they dig in and feed for hours to days, with the time frame dependent on the species. Careful "tick checks" should be performed at least twice a day in tick-infested country, and early removal of embedded ticks prevents the transmission of many diseases. They should be removed gently with tweezers, without excess squeezing, by taking hold of the tick as near the skin as possible with the tweezers perpendicular to the tick's body, and pulling straight out. Any other removal method increases the risk of germ transmission. Wash the little wound. A swipe with an antiseptic may be useful. Watch for signs of illness—rash, fever, flu-like symptoms—which should send you to a doctor as soon as possible.

Snakes

There are two types of snakes you want to avoid:

Pit vipers (rattlesnake, water moccasin, copperhead) bite with either or both of their retractable fangs, and their bites produce immediate local pain and swelling within approximately fifteen minutes. Blister formation and discoloration usually occur, and the bite may lead to local skin destruction. The bitten often report lip tingling and a funny taste within an hour or so. Muscle twitching may result. Death is unusual.

Coral snakes have relatively dull fangs, so they have to gnaw a few moments to deposit venom. Burning pain at the bite site is often followed by pain, tingling, or numbness extending up from the bite—but these signs and symptoms may take up to twelve hours to develop. Serious systemic manifestations include difficulty speaking, swallowing, seeing, and breathing. Bites from these snakes are much less common but much more dangerous.

Just the Facts: Prevention of Snake Bites

1. Do not try to pick up or otherwise capture a snake.
2. Check places you intend to put your hands and feet before exposing any body part to a bite, especially in the dark.
3. Gather firewood before dark, or use a flashlight and gather carefully after dark.
4. In snake country, keep your tent zipped closed.
5. Wear high, thick boots and/or gaiters while traveling in dangerous snake country.
6. When passing a snake, stay out of striking range, which is about one-half the snake's length.
7. If you hear the "buzz" of a rattler, freeze, find it with your eyes without moving your head, wait for it to relax the strike position, and back away slowly.

If a Snake Bites

After any snakebite, follow this advice:

1. Get away from the snake.
2. Remain as calm as possible.
3. Remove anything that might restrict circulation, such as rings, before swelling occurs.
4. Gently wash the bite site.
5. Splint the bitten arm or leg, and keep the bite site level with the heart.
6. Find a doctor as quickly as possibly.
7. Do not use cold packs, tourniquets, cutting and sucking, or electrical shocks.

Common Problems

Cuts and scrapes send you looking for the first-aid kit most often. Then there's the possibility of a sprained ankle or knee, and occasionally a bone that could be broken. You want to be sure your first aid is appropriate, and you want to know when the injury needs a doctor's care.

Wounds

When an open wound is the problem, three goals are worthy of consideration:

1. *Stop serious bleeding.* Almost all bleeding can be stopped with direct pressure and elevation: pressure from your hand directly on the wound and elevation of the wound above the bleeder's heart. If you have enough time, place a sterile dressing

on the wound before applying pressure. When immediate action is critical, grab anything absorbent to press into the wound. Keep in mind that you can sometimes let small wounds bleed to a stop, a process that may actually clean them a bit.

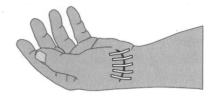

A closed wound

2. *Prevent infection.* Proper wound cleaning, closing, and dressing will prevent infection in most small wounds. Cleaning also speeds healing and reduces scarring. The best method for cleaning is mechanical irrigation. Irrigation involves a high-pressure stream of an acceptable solution that is best directed into the wound from an irrigation syringe. The best cleaning solution is plain uninfected water—water, in other words, that's safe to drink. Draw the solution into the syringe, hold it 2 to 4 inches above and perpendicular to the wound, and push down forcefully on the plunger. Keep the wound tipped so the solution runs out. Use at least half a liter, and more if the wound still looks unclean. If you don't have an irrigation syringe, you can improvise by using a biking water bottle, melting a pinhole in the center of the lid of a standard water bottle, or punching a pinhole in a clean plastic bag.

3. *Promote healing.* Promote healing with proper dressings and bandages. The primary covering of a wound is the *dressing.* Sterile, nonadherent, porous, bacteria-resistant, and easy-to-use dressings are best. Wounds heal faster with less scarring if they are kept slightly moist with an antibiotic ointment or with a dressing that holds in the body's moisture while keeping out external moisture. The dressing should completely cover the wound, and ideally it will extend a half inch or so beyond the wound's edge. You will not have the ideal dressing available unless you pack it in a first-aid kit.

The function of the *bandage* is to fix, protect, and further assist the dressing. It can be conforming gauze, tape, elastic wraps, clean cotton strips, or something improvised out of anything available. For very small wounds, the dressing and the bandage are available as a unit, often called adhesive strips, and are found in all first-aid kits.

First Aid and Medical Care: Treating Abrasions

Unlike deeper wounds, abrasions (scrapes) are best when cleaned initially by scrubbing them. Use of an anesthetic cleansing pad prior to scrubbing can ease the pain a little, but be prepared for reports of distress from the one being scrubbed. Scrub with a scrub brush, a sponge impregnated with green soap or another antimicrobial, or a gauze pad and soap and water. Irrigate until the wound is clean. Apply a thin layer of antibiotic ointment, and then a dressing and a bandage.

Burns

First and foremost, stop the burning process—and the faster the better. Burns can continue to cause harm long after the flames are out. Cool the burn with water until the pain is gone. Do not try to remove hot plastic or anything else melted into the burn. Then follow these general guidelines:

1. Gently wash the burn with soap and water. Pat dry.
2. Remove the skin of blisters that have popped open—but do not open closed blisters.
3. Dress the burn with a thin layer of antibiotic ointment.
4. Cover the burn with a gauze pad, a layer of roll gauze, or clean clothing.
5. If you have no ointment, no dressings, and/or no skill, leave the burn alone. The burn's surface will dry into a scablike covering that provides a significant amount of protection.

Blisters

Blisters, usually developing on the foot, are mild burns caused by friction. Friction produces a separation of the tough outer layer of skin from the sensitive inner layer. Blisters range from unpleasant to terribly debilitating. Once the bubble develops, draining blisters is far better than having them rupture inside a dirty sock. Clean around the site thoroughly. Sterilize the point of a needle or knife, and gently open the blister. Massage out the fluid. Leaving the roof of the blister intact will make it feel better and heal faster. If the roof has been rubbed away, treat the wound as you would any other, but include a dressing that limits friction, such as a piece of moleskin with a hole cut in the center (fill the hole with a lubricating ointment). Another piece of moleskin or tape over the hole will keep the ointment in place.

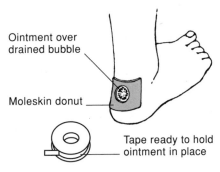

Ointment over drained bubble

Moleskin donut

Tape ready to hold ointment in place

Patching a blister

Sprains

Sprains are injuries to ligaments, the bands holding bones to bones at joints. The injury can vary from small to very large. First aid for sprains is RICE: Rest, Ice, Compression, and Elevation. Do not use the injury (Rest) for the first half hour or so while you reduce its temperature (Ice) as much as possible without freezing the tissue. Without ice or a chemical cold pack, soak the joint in cold water or wrap it in wet cotton and let evaporation cool the damaged area. Fit an elastic bandage snugly around the sprain (Compression) but not tight enough to cut off healthy circulation. Keep the injury higher than your heart (Elevation)—if you are the injured person, of course. After twenty to thirty minutes of RICE, remove the elastic bandage and let the joint warm naturally for ten to fifteen minutes before use. (*Note:* the injury will heal faster if RICE is repeated often until pain and swelling subside.)

TIP

SPRAIN OR BROKEN BONE?: If you think the injury is a sprain, but it hurts a lot to use it, even after RICE, suspect a broken bone and find a doctor.

Diarrhea

Diarrhea is the most common illness disturbing the camping life. It has many causes, but whatever the cause, dehydration is the immediate problem with diarrhea. Mild diarrhea can be treated with water or diluted fruit juices or sports drinks. Persistent diarrhea requires more aggressive replacement of electrolytes lost in the stool. Oral rehydration solutions are best for treating serious diarrhea. You can get by, usually, adding one teaspoon of salt and eight teaspoons of sugar to a liter of water. The sufferer should drink about one-quarter of this solution every hour, along with all the water he or she will tolerate. Rice, grains, bananas, and potatoes are okay to eat. Fats, dairy products, caffeine, and alcohol should be avoided. Anti-diarrheal drugs should be considered for your first-aid kit. If the diarrhea is not under control in twenty-four to seventy-two hours, the best trail leads to a doctor.

Environmental Hazards

Although you might say—and reasonably so—that the "environment" is a large part of what attracted you to camp, that same environment—with its heat, cold, and intense sunlight—can also challenge your body.

Heat Illness

Heat can cause a wide range of problems: everything from feeling hot and tired to life-threatening heat stroke.

1. *Heat Exhaustion.* With a lot of internal water sweated out, along with salt, you can feel like you are having a sudden attack of flu: unusual fatigue, headache, nausea, dizziness. You are experiencing a volume problem—not enough water inside—and it is typically not serious, as long as you take care of the problem right away. The cure is suggested by the name of the condition: exhaustion calls for rest, preferably in a cool, shady spot. Replace lost fluids with water, and replace lost salt by adding a pinch to a liter of water or munching salty snacks. To increase the rate of cooling, you can be wet down and fanned. If you feel drowsy, take a nap. When you feel okay, you may continue the adventure—but continue drinking water.

2. *Heat Stroke.* With heat stroke your body is making heat faster than it is shedding it. If the heat rises too high, your brain cooks—and you die. Disorientation and bizarre personality changes are common signs. Skin turns hot and red and sometimes (but far from always) dry. You are experiencing a temperature problem from too much internal heat. Only rapid cooling will save you. Heat-retaining clothing must be removed, and you must be drenched with water. Cooling efforts, with a shortage of water, should be concentrated on the head and neck. Constant fanning increases evaporation and, therefore, speeds cooling. Massage of the limbs to encourage cooler blood to return to the core is beneficial. Even if you return to what seems normal, the bad things high heat does to the inside of you might last for the rest of your life—and you need a doctor's care immediately.

PREVENTION OF HEAT ILLNESS:

* Stay well hydrated. An indication of adequate hydration is urine output that is clear and relatively copious.
* Munch on lightly salted snacks.
* Wear baggy, loosely woven clothing that allows evaporation of sweat. Keep your head shaded.
* Keep yourself trim. Overweight people are more susceptible to heat illnesses.
* Allow time for acclimatization when you are new to a hot environment. Go slow the first few days and avoid exposure during the hottest times of day.
* Beware of drugs, such as antihistamines, that increase your risk of heat illness.
* Rest often in the shade, especially if the humidity is high.

TIP

Cold Illness

Loss of heat from the core of your body causes the condition known as *hypothermia*, which can be, for simplicity, divided into mild and severe problems:

- With *mild hypothermia,* you can talk, eat, and shiver. Change the environment so the heat being produced internally by shivering is not lost. Get out of wet clothes and into something dry, out of wind and cold and into some kind of shelter, even if the only shelter available is the protection of waterproof, windproof clothing. Cover your head and neck where critical heat is easily lost. Protect yourself from the cold ground. Replace fuel for your metabolism. Fluids are more important than solids when you're cold. A warm (not hot) sweet drink will add a tiny bit of heat and a lot of simple sugar for energy. Even cold fluids are better than no fluids. Stay dry and warm until you return to normal, and then you can continue your camping trip.
- With *severe hypothermia,* you are semi-conscious or unconscious, and you have stopped shivering. You seriously need help. You must be handled with *extreme gentleness*—no rough movement. Clothing should be removed, and you should be bundled in layers of dry insulation that shield you thoroughly from the cold ground. Hot water bottles or heat packs placed in dry socks or shirts and other appropriate places on your body—chest, armpits, groin—will be of benefit. Finish with a vapor barrier—a tent fly, a sheet of plastic, garbage bags—something to trap any heat remaining inside. The final product is a cocoon, a "hypothermia wrap" open only to the mouth and nose. You need a doctor as soon as possible.

TIPS

SIGNS OF HYPOTHERMIA:
- *The "umbles."* Stumbling, grumbling, fumbling, mumbling are early signs.
- *A brain dulled by the cold.* Dropping gear without noticing, losing direction without caring, feeling cold and doing nothing about it are also early signs.
- *Shivering that may become uncontrollable.* This sign develops later and may indicate a more serious problem.
- *The cessation of shivering without a return to a normal level of consciousness.* This is a later and very serious sign.

PREVENTION OF HYPOTHERMIA:
- Wear clothing that retains body heat even when wet.
- Stay dry by wearing layers of clothing, taking off layers before sweating starts, and putting them on again before cooling occurs.
- Drink lots of water.
- Eat lots, especially carbohydrates.
- Maintain a pace that prevents overexertion. Rest often.
- In a group, watch each other for the early signs of hypothermia—and treat it early.

Solar Radiation

The sun radiates a range of light that includes, on the short end of the spectrum, ultraviolet light (UV). Short-term overexposure to UV radiation burns skin. Prolonged exposure, over years, leads to premature skin aging and degenerative skin disorders such as skin cancer. First aid for sunburn includes cooling the skin, applying a moisturizer, ibuprofen for pain and inflammation, and staying out of direct sunlight. If blisters form, a doctor should be consulted.

PREVENTION OF SUNBURN:

- Limit your exposure to direct sunlight.
- Wear tightly woven clothing.
- Wear a hat with a wide brim.
- Wear sunscreen with an SPF of at least 15. SPF 30 is better.
- If you're especially sensitive to UV light, wear a sunblock, such as zinc oxide.

TIP

Just the Facts: UV Light

1. Clouds provide some shade but very little UV protection. On a bright day with fluffy cumulus clouds dotting the sky, you can actually receive an increased dose of ultraviolet B radiation (UVB)—as much as 15 percent more—because scattered UV is reflected down to the ground by clouds. Only thick, dark rain clouds offer much UV protection.
2. UV radiation is most intense between the hours of 10:00 AM and 3:00 PM.
3. Summer sunshine is more harmful even though the sun in winter is closer to Earth. In summer the sun is more directly overhead. UV levels peak in most of the United States around mid-July.
4. Reflection of UV light can be substantial. Grass reflects only 2 to 3 percent, and sand reflects 20 to 30 percent. Snow and ice, in comparison, reflect 80 to 90 percent. Water can reflect 100 percent of the UV light striking its surface. In the mid-morning and mid-afternoon, when the sun's rays strike at a 35- to 45-degree angle, water's reflectivity reaches its maximum.
5. Latitude changes mean UV radiation changes due to differing angles of sunlight. Equatorial locations receive the most sunshine. Skin cancer rates in Texas and Florida, according to the National Institutes of Health, are approximately twice the rates of Wisconsin and Montana.
6. Wind by itself does not "burn" skin, but the combination of wind and UV radiation intensifies skin damage. Wind dries skin, removing the natural protection of urocanic acid. Wind irritates skin, making sunburns worse. Wind cools skin, allowing longer periods of exposure without discomfort. In wind, in other words, you can burn without feeling as much heat on your skin.

Poison Ivy, Oak, and Sumac

Everyone should be made aware of, and taught how to identify and avoid, all poisonous plants. Campsites should be checked closely for the presence of poison oak, sumac, or ivy. If contact is suspected, all skin that may have contacted a poisonous plant should be washed immediately with soft soap and cold water. You can wash off the oil that causes the reaction before it soaks in and produces the reaction. Clothing and shoes that may have contacted the poisonous plant should be cleaned thoroughly. If the itch, redness, and fluid-filled bumps of a reaction to a plant develop on skin, calamine lotion will ease the itch, but a reaction takes seven to ten days to completely subside.

Poison ivy: leaves of three, let it be.

9

CAMP ACTIVITIES

A couple of quiet days and nights away from your everyday life may be all you're after. Even if camping is all you do, immense joy can be had from that experience alone. But tent and vehicle camping provides numerous opportunities, depending on where you camp, to enjoy camp-related activities. In addition to visitor centers, nature centers, museums, and historical sites, approximately one-half of campers take day hikes and one-half go for bike rides. You may have a chance to paddle, swim, lure a fish onto a hook, or contentedly watch wildlife. You may decide to hone your photography skills. And who knows what else? This chapter will give you some ideas and some guidelines.

{ In the Words of a Sage }

Pantanjali, Buddha, Moses and Jesus did not go to workshops or seminars or even churches. They went directly to nature: sat under a Bodhi tree or on top of a mountain or in a cave. We've been living off the residual remains of their inspiration for thousands of years, but this has about run out. It is time to return to the source of this inspiration—the earth itself.

—*Dolores Lachapelle*

Hiking

A walk in the mountains, a ramble through a forest, wandering in a desert, exploring a beach—no matter where you set camp, hiking will be an option. With no special equipment required, hiking will be the easiest of camp activities. In most cases, everyone can be involved, from youngest to oldest, regardless of ability. There is so much more to be seen than what you see from your campsite, and walking is an extremely healthy form of exercise.

Nature Trails

Sometimes the hike will be along a nature trail, a well-maintained pathway, often enriched with numerous signs relating the natural history and, perhaps, the human history of the area. You'll enjoy a walk while learning about the trees, animals, and rocks specific to the locale. Often brochures at the trailhead or at a visitor center will describe the hike in detail. The trail will be very easy to follow—and it will usually be a loop, ending at or near its starting point.

Striking Out on Your Own

If you're headed away from camp on your own, you'll want to gather more information and prepare more thoroughly. The farther you intend to roam, the more information you'll want to have at hand and the more time and effort you'll want to put into preparation.

Following the signs on the Desert Nature Trail, Arches National Park

Off to see the world

Sources of Information

• An accurate map is the best place to start. A topographical map will provide the most information about the terrain: the ups, the downs, the meadows, the rivers, the towering peaks. If you don't know how to read a topo map, it will be well worth your time to learn (see "Topo Map Basics"). Studying a topo map can be an adventure in its own right—an armchair adventure, but an adventure all the same.

- Guidebooks offer a lot of valuable data.
- You also can gather a wealth of information from campground managers, rangers, and maybe your neighbors about the specifics of a trail.

ABOUT YOUR DESTINATION: You may find the most contentment just walking in wild land, but you'll often enjoy anticipating your arrival at a pond, a waterfall, a footbridge over a chasm, or a high point with an expansive view, even seeing a moose feeding in the shallows of a Maine lake.

Trail Tips

1. *Tell someone who will remain in camp where you're going and when you plan to return.* A campsite neighbor or a camp manager is a good choice for this safety measure. If you are disabled or lost, they'll know to send help.

2. *Anticipate a change in the weather.* In mountains, for example, an afternoon rainstorm can sweep over a ridge and hide the clouds in what seems only a moment. A desert hike will turn remarkably chilly when the sun drops below the horizon. Everyone should have an extra layer of clothing, a hat, and raingear. Raingear should have a hood to protect the head, even if what you choose is only an inexpensive, disposable poncho.

3. *Be realistic when you decide how far to hike,* keeping in mind the fitness and age of all hikers in your group. A lake might lie four miles away, but it might have been a long time since you walked four miles on rough terrain. Then there are the four miles back!

4. *Be realistic when you choose how fast to hike.* Here's an old outdoor leadership guideline: a group travels at the pace of its slowest member. Anyone expending extra energy just to keep up will have less fun—and fun, said Dr. Seuss, is good. Those trying to keep up will also increase their risk of harm from fatigue or blisters.

5. *Slow and steady wins the race.* Start out at a slow pace, giving your body the opportunity to warm up and loosen up. When the trail runs steeply downhill, take shorter steps. Long, plunging, downhill steps stress your muscles and joints, giving them a beating they don't need. It is far less tiring to take short steps, and most hiking accidents occur when hikers are walking down steep terrain. If the trail turns up steeply, it's safe to take long strides, but once again shorter steps require less energy. Pace yourself, and gain altitude at a stride that does not take your breath away.

6. *Step over obstacles.* It takes less energy to step over obstacles such as rocks and logs than to step up onto them—but keep an eye out for hidden creatures.

7. *Carry water, and don't forget to drink it.* Remind yourself to drink, and remind any children with you. Dehydration burns up your energy, reduces

your coordination, can give you a headache, and threatens the wonder of the experience. An adult needs three to four liters of fluid for a daylong hike. A healthy rule of thumb is to drink enough to prevent thirst. If you can't remember when you last urinated, you're probably dehydrated. If your last urination was dark yellow, you're definitely dehydrated.

8. *Whatever the length of your hike, rest often.* Sit. Have a drink of water. Take in the view. Smell the wild roses. You'll carry more memories home, and you'll also arrive refreshed from your walk.

ELEVATION CHANGES ADD MILES: Remember that elevation gain adds to the miles of a hike. Every 1000 feet of elevation gain adds a mile or so to the energy required to do the hike. A waterfall that is five trail miles away and 1000 feet of altitude higher will be the equivalent of a six-mile-plus hike.

The Ten Essentials

To be safest, every group should be carrying the Ten Essentials, a list of items devised by professionals after many years of experience. You may have them and not need them, but how tragic to need them and not have them.

Ten Essentials: A Systems Approach

1. Navigation (map and compass)—including a map of the local area, of course.
2. Sun protection (sunglasses and sunscreen).
3. Insulation (extra clothing)—in case the mercury dips, the wind rises, the rain falls.
4. Illumination (headlamp or flashlight)—and extra batteries.
5. First-aid supplies—and knowing how to use them.
6. Fire (firestarter and matches/lighter).
7. Repair kit and tools (including knife)—a small, folding knife works just fine.
8. Nutrition (extra food)—could be granola bars, could be a full-on picnic lunch.
9. Hydration (extra water)—and don't forget to drink it.
10. Emergency shelter—a poncho will serve in a pinch.

DAY PACKS—TO EACH HIS OR HER OWN:

- Everything a group needs can be carried in a large day pack.
- It's not critical, but it's nice if all hikers have their own packs—and then the packs can be smaller. Personal packs keep one person from bearing the load of the group, and they add a sense of self-reliance to all members of the party.
- Children with a small day pack, appropriately packed, will have what they need to stay as safe as possible if they're separated from their parents (see Chapter 5).

- Packs are not created equal. To maximize comfort, and increase enjoyment, make sure your pack fits your body.
- Padded shoulder straps and a padded hip belt will greatly reduce the strain of carrying a pack. These are, however, not required.
- Durable, coated fabrics will last longer and repel a light rain.
- A top-loading pack is more water resistant because it has only one opening, but you'll have to dig down inside to find what you want. A panel-loading pack provides easier access to the items inside due to its long zipper and horseshoe shape and is my preference.
- Fill your pack with the soft items—such as raingear and extra clothes—against your back. Keep the hard items away from your body.

You can carry all you need in a day pack.

TOPO MAP BASICS:

1. Before leaving camp, orient the map. You need a compass to orient a map. Find north with the compass. Point the top of the map to north. Now your map is basically oriented. Each time you stop on the trail to check your location, orient the map to north.
2. Before leaving camp, find your location on the map. It is difficult, sometimes impossible, to find your location if you don't know where you started.
3. Trails, rough roads, and boundary lines are black. Trace your intended line of travel with your finger and your eyes.
4. The color green typically represents heavy vegetation (usually a forest).
5. White means little or no vegetation (including meadows).
6. Blue is water.
7. Look for landmarks on the map—creeks, bridges, lakes, meadows, cliffs— and watch for the same geographical features as you hike.
8. The contour lines swirling across a topo map connect points of equal elevation. The spaces between contour lines are called contour intervals, and they represent the vertical distance between the lines. When the contour

lines are spaced widely apart, the terrain rises or falls gently. When the contour lines are almost on top of each other, you'll find a cliff face.

9. Every fifth contour line is a darker color, and, somewhere on that line, you will find a number telling you the actual elevation above sea level that the line represents. The accuracy of contour lines, however, depends upon how far apart they are—and not all maps are the same. If 500 feet separate two darker lines, for example, and four lighter lines stand between the darker lines, separating the space between the darker lines into five sections, then the contour interval for that map is 100 feet. Contour intervals may be as short as 10 feet. The smaller the intervals, the greater the detail. With large intervals, significant terrain changes may not show on the map.

10. Find the elevation of your starting point and your ending point, and you'll know how much elevation you'll gain or lose. Watch for significant gains and losses of elevation along the way.

Planning a hike with map and compass

FEET VERSUS METERS: Some maps list elevations in meters instead of feet. Here's the conversion: *1 meter = 3.3 feet.*

TIP

{ **Personal Reflections** }

An old trail guideline says a child can hike the same number of miles as his or her age. A five-year-old, then, might hike five miles. After countless trips with my children, I have decided the old guideline ain't necessarily so. When my son was five, I felt fortunate if he walked two-and-a-half miles of a five-mile hike. He spent a lot of time on my shoulders. Still, I'd do all those miles with him again without even thinking about it.

TIP

EXTENDING A CHILD'S MILES: With small children, you can extend a hike with a child-carrier that rides on an adult's shoulders like a backpack. Jack Wolfskin's Watchtower is an excellent example: a child-carrier comfortable for adult and child, adjustable to fit as the child grows, and including ample gear-carrying capacity.

Biking

Almost everybody can ride a bike. Even if years have passed since you pedaled, it's something you just don't forget how to do. In addition to being easy, bike riding is great exercise, and you'll get to check the lay of the land for many miles around your campsite. Bikes can turn an idle camping trip into an excellent adventure.

Mountain Bikes

For someone on a bike, the world lies divided into two parts—the part you

Mama Kristin Speaks

A great hiking game for kids: devise a treasure hunt! Give each child a large zip-top baggie and a list of items to find: a pinecone, a bug, a white rock, a flower, an acorn, a bottle cap, a red or yellow leaf (in fall), a berry, and so on.

can ride your bike across and the part you can't. If you want to increase the size of the part you *can* ride across, choose a mountain bike. Although mountain bikes and their counterparts, road bikes, differ in several important ways, the big difference is this: mountain bikes can go more places. Mountain bikes are made for rough trails (and smooth trails), for shallow creek crossings, for rock hopping, log jumping, and mud sliding. Two things will stop a mountain bike: (a) geography—such as raging rivers and steep cliffs, and (b) signs that say something like "No Bikes Allowed." You will also choose not to ride across fragile terrain—say, a meadow of wildflowers—because of the damage you'll do.

Ready to ride

BIKE RENTALS: If you don't own a bike, often you will be able to rent one from outfitters near campgrounds—and, occasionally, from the campground itself. Check ahead.

BIKING GEAR:
- *A helmet.* Everyone needs one for safety.
- *Sunglasses.* These are not required, but most bikers are happier wearing a pair. They shut out the glare and keep grit out of your eyes.
- *Specialized biking gear and clothing.* Though available, these are not required: gloves, padded shorts, and biking shoes. Just loose shorts or pants, a shirt, a pair of sneakers, and you're ready to ride.

Buying a Bike
When you decide to purchase a bike, you will, as you suspect, be faced with many choices. You can spend $100 or, if you get excited, $2,000. As with other gear-related choices, a reputable bike dealer will take you a long way down the road to knowledge.
- To make your riding experiences as happy as possible, *the bike must fit.* Every different bike, even bikes the same size, will ride differently. A bike dealer will

help you choose a size, but you won't know for sure if a bike fits until you put a mile or so of pedaling behind you.

- You may be happy with a single-speed bike: one chain ring in front, one chain in back. After you ride awhile, though, *you'll almost always end up wanting more gears.* A twenty-one-speed, for example, with three chain rings in front and seven in back, offers low gears for laboring up the steepest inclines to high gears for fast-paced flat-terrain riding.

You never forget how to ride a bike.

- You may choose rear *shock absorbers* or front and rear shock absorbers to help smooth out rough terrain.
- You may prefer *a special and more comfortable seat* to replace the off-the-rack seat.

KNOW YOUR LIMITS: Match your ability to the terrain. Stick to roads and easy trails at first. As your ability improves, attempt more rugged rides cautiously. Save the steep downhill runs, jumps, and water crossings until you're an accomplished biker.

Paddling

From many campsites you'll hear the Siren call of water, the lure of lakes and meandering rivers begging to be explored with boat and paddle. Why not heed the call? Shoving off in a canoe will add a wondrous new dimension to camping.

1. First and foremost, for safety's sake, everyone in the boat should know how to swim.
2. Second, no matter how powerful a swimming stroke anybody possesses, everyone should wear a personal flotation device (PFD). A sudden, unexpected immersion in water, especially cold water, has spelled doom for more than one expert swimmer. And every paddler, no matter how expert, has flipped a canoe.
3. With canoe and paddle ready, PFD nearby, set the boat in the water and load it there. That means your feet get wet, but you don't want to drag a loaded boat across sand and rocks, potentially damaging the hull.
4. Step slowly into the center of a canoe, keeping your center of gravity low, with the least amount of side-to-side shifting.
5. Before shoving off, check the "trim"—how level the craft floats in the water. Canoes excessively weighted in the bow (front) or stern (rear) will be difficult to steer, and one loaded excessively to port (left) or starboard (right) will be tippy. You can shift around gear and people to perfect the trim.

Basic Strokes

With five different strokes—the forward, the J-stroke, the back, the draw, and the pry—and with practice, you can make a canoe do everything but fly.

- *The forward stroke.* Reaching forward with the paddle, you dip it in the water and pull the water back

Water Sports: About PFDs

Unlike the old days, you can find modern PFDs that are light and comfortable—but most important is fit. A well-fitted PFD is snug. You can slip out of a loose one if you plunge into water. Small children should wear PFDs with a strap running between the legs that prevents them from riding out of the flotation device.

Getting ready to paddle

along the side of the canoe. Remember that every forward stroke not only propels the canoe forward but also turns it away from the side you're paddling on. Novice paddlers will compensate for the turn by switching the stroke from one side to the other side of the canoe—and that works.

- *The J-stroke.* Better paddlers incorporate the J-stroke into their paddling skills. For a J-stroke, perform a forward stroke, but at the end of the stroke turn the paddle blade slightly away from the canoe and gently curl the end of the forward stroke away from the canoe. If you gently pry the paddle off the gunwale—the upper edge of the canoe's side—to complete the J-stroke, you'll perform a more powerful yet less tiring J. With practice, and it does take practice, you can keep a canoe on a straight track without ever switching sides.
- *The backstroke.* A backstroke is the reverse of a forward stroke. A backstroke turns the canoe toward the side you're paddling on, so you can use it to steer, but you lose forward momentum when you backstroke to turn the canoe.
- *The draw stroke.* For a draw stroke, reach out and away from the canoe with the paddle, dip it in the water, and draw the water toward the canoe. You can use the draw for maneuvering, such as docking. The draw also can be used to

steer the canoe with very little loss of forward momentum.

- *The pry stroke.* For a pry stroke, dip the paddle in the water near the canoe and push the water away from the canoe, prying the paddle off the gunwale for power. The pry can be used for close maneuvering and also for steering.

Buying a Canoe

If thoughts of paddling intrigue you, don't rush out and buy a boat. As with other more expensive gear, borrow or rent until you have paddled enough to make a sound choice. When you decide to purchase a canoe, each will have a price tag to match the quality. You can buy a tough, serviceable canoe from Coleman for about $300, and on the other end of the price range you can have an excellent Kevlar canoe from Mad River for about $2,600. A dealer can explain in detail the many aspects of canoe design, and as you develop as a paddler you'll come to appreciate the finer qualities of a well-designed and well-constructed canoe.

Canoe Lengths

Canoes come in differing lengths (see "Water Sports: Equipment Basics"). The longer the boat, generally speaking, the more weight, and therefore the more people, it can carry. The longer the boat, the faster it will move across the water. And finally, the longer the boat, still speaking generally, the slower it will turn.

Hull Designs

A canoe with a deep-V hull will turn faster than a shallow-V hull, but the shallow-V design offers more stability. Since you'll seldom need a fast turn, unless you take up white-water paddling, a relatively flat hull will be your best choice.

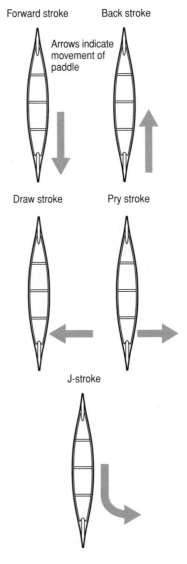

Basic canoe strokes

Canoe Composition

Canoes may be constructed of aluminum, wood and canvas, fiberglass, or a lightweight composite—each with advantages and disadvantages. Aluminum is typically less expensive, but it dents and bends somewhat easily. Composite is the lightest and strongest, as well as the most expensive. Fiberglass usually falls in between.

Water Sports: Equipment Basics

PADDLES: You'll want to try different types of paddles. Wide-bladed paddles push more water, so you move faster, but they require more energy than narrow blades. Bent-shaft paddles will cost more, but they require the least energy if you plan a long day in the boat.

CANOE LOAD LIMITS: Know the load limit of your canoe, and stay within the limits. Overloaded boats are far easier to flip.

CANOE LENGTHS:
- Short canoes, about 14 to 15 feet, are designed for one adult.
- Canoes about 16 feet long are designed for two adults.
- Canoes about 17 feet long will usually carry three adults.
- Long canoes, 18 feet or more, will usually carry four adults.

Getting ready to catch the Big One.

{ Personal Reflections }

I love canoeing. I find myself choosing a campsite because it's near great paddling instead of choosing to paddle because my campsite is near water. I canoe camp, too, shoving off with everything I need and more for a few days or a week. I talked my wife into a canoeing honeymoon—and we're still married. But canoe camping is another story, similar to this one but worthy of another book.

Fishing

The grandest goal of fishing is to enjoy the experience. It's typically a lovely setting, quiet, and worthy of contemplation. It's as if you have become one with the breeze, the shore, the water, and perhaps later the finned fellow earthling—a Zen thing. Of course you may not care about all that. You may just want a fish for dinner.

{ Personal Reflections }

I started out with a cane pole, to which I tied a line, to which I attached a bobber and a hook, on which I impaled a worm or cricket. There will never be a numerical accounting of the hours I spent thus occupied—nor an accounting of the value to my spirit. But I came to this understanding later in life. I learned to fish, at a very early age, from my father, and we had a very specific goal: to catch a lot of fish.

The goal should be to enjoy the experience.

Fishing Gear

1. *Spincasting.* If you're new to fishing, choose a short rod with an enclosed reel. The line is inside the reel, and it releases when you cast forward and lift your thumb off a push button. When you start to reel in, the line automatically catches within the reel. It's a simple outfit, easily handled by small children. You can buy one of these spincasting outfits for very little money—but don't buy too cheaply. Inexpensive models may not last as long as your camping trip. If you enjoy fishing, you can choose later to move up to longer rods and more sophisticated spin- or bait-casting reels that demand more time and practice to master.

2. *Fly-fishing.* The most challenging and satisfying form of angling is fly-fishing. In spincasting, the weight of the lure or bait carries it far out into the water with little effort. In fly-fishing, the ephemeral weight of the line carries the practically weightless fly out to settle lightly on the water. It is, in short, difficult to master fly-fishing. The rewards, however, are extreme. You can teach yourself to spincast, picking up pointers from angling neighbors, but you'll need to sit at, or stand near, the feet of an accomplished fly-fishing expert to learn that art.

3. *Hook, line, and sinker.* There are at least a million things to attach to your rod and reel—the lines, the lures, the hooks, the baits, the sinkers, the bobbers. When you start out, tell a dealer where you're going and what you hope to catch there. To know this, you'll have to do a little research. She or he will be able to tell you what you need.

THE VALUE OF EXPERIENCE: Other anglers may offer a chance for you to learn more about fishing. Take advantage of every opportunity.

Whereyacastin'?

Successful anglers—meaning the ones who catch fish—know where to fish. In still or in moving water, cast where fish are most likely to be.

1. *Still water.* Fish feeding in lakes or other still water will swim around looking for food. Watch the surface for awhile before casting randomly into the water. If you see fish feeding from the surface, fish there, and keep your lure or bait on or near the surface. If they're feeding deep, drop your lure or bait down to them.

2. *Moving water.* Fish feeding in streams and rivers will wait for food to come to them, carried by the current. Because it takes energy to hold a position in moving water, fish will wait in places where the current flows most easily, in pools or downstream from rocks and logs. Fish will also wait near "seams" in moving water, places where faster-moving water meets slower-moving water. You can see seams, for example, where water rushes around a large

boulder and then enters a deep pool, and where a fast-moving stream enters a slower-moving river. Fish will wait in the slower water for the nearby faster current to carry food to them.

Whatchacatchin'?
Successful anglers know something about the fish they're after. Fish fall generally into two categories:

1. *Active feeders.* Fish who are feeding may be really hungry, consuming anything that looks edible. Or they may be only slightly hungry—and frustratingly so for you—taking a small nibble and spitting out the rest when the food is not especially appealing. The nibblers require greater attention to your line, and a quick pull on the rod when a fish is nibbling. Fish, even hungry fish, may be amazingly particular, choosing to eat only certain types of food. For that reason, if you haven't had a bite after a couple of dozen casts, change your lure or bait. Fish may watch disinterestedly as a silver spoon flutters by, then bite ferociously when a golden spinner zips past.

2. *Resting fish.* After eating enough, fish rest. You can catch fish that have already fed, occasionally, if you're "lucky," but you want to go after feeding fish.

FISH THE SHADOWS: When a choice presents itself, fish show a preference for shadows, feeling less vulnerable than in bright light.

Viewing Wildlife
Of all that you see on your camping trip, few experiences (if any) will match the joy of viewing wild animals. You may spot a raccoon poking around the garbage cans in daylight or a deer passing silently through the shadows a few paces from your breakfast table, but those who see the most wildlife go looking for wildlife.

1. *You see wildlife by going where the wild things are.* Natural history books and/or rangers will tell you about the specific habits of specific animals, and the more you know about animals the more likely you are to see them. The memorable sightings seldom occur without planning.

2. *Generally speaking, wild animals feed at night and rest safely hidden during the day.* You can usually find them, however, late in the evening, getting an early start, or early in the morning, getting to bed late.

3. *If you're out to see animals, you must walk slowly and quietly, paying close attention.* Most animals will see you and hear you long before you see them. If you're upwind, they'll also smell you long before you see them. The fact that they know you're there doesn't necessarily mean they'll run away. Fast, noisy hikers seldom see animals, partly because the animals are startled and flee, and partly because you're walking too fast to pay close attention.

4. *Not only should you walk slowly, but you should stop completely every few steps.* Look closely into the forest, up the open slopes, or along waterways.
5. *Look behind you.* The deer family—including moose and elk—seem to enjoy watching you pass, then stepping lightly onto the trail behind you.
6. *You may see an animal, but you're more likely to see part of an animal first:* a set of antlers above a fallen tree, a furry ear in tall grass.
7. *Watch for movement.* If you think you see movement, stand still and stare quietly until the animal, if it is one, moves again. To see the most wildlife, you have to be more patient than the animals.
8. *You will see more wildlife and more detail with binoculars* (see below). You can examine the forest and meadows more closely with binoculars, and you can observe animals better from a distance. The animals you get to watch the longest will usually be a long way off anyway. They don't typically stand still when you're nearby.

WILDLIFE VIEWING SAFETY: *Be warned:* every year a few wildlife watchers are injured, sometimes seriously, by wildlife. Those injured always break the cardinal rule by getting too close. Wild animals, even national park animals that have grown accustomed to tourists, need distance to feel safe. Get too close to them, and they'll either run away or charge. Getting close enough to startle animals into fleeing is unhealthy for the animals. Getting close enough to stir up a charge can be unhealthy for you. Any animal that stares intently at you with ears turned your way is concerned—and you are close enough. Any animal that moves away from you is deeply concerned—and you are too close. Any animal with babies will be protective, and she may charge. Even deer have charged humans to protect their fawns. Any male in the fall rutting season should be treated with great respect. He may charge if he feels the slightest threat to his domain. Enjoy wildlife, yes, but give wild animals the distance they need.

Binoculars

Any binoculars are better than no binoculars, but when you pay more you'll get more. If you enjoy watching wildlife, buy the best optics you can afford. Inexpensive binoculars are more likely to give you a distorted picture, and they're almost guaranteed to give you more eyestrain. A small pair will be lighter, of course, but a big pair of glasses will give you a bigger picture with, once again, less eyestrain. As a ball-park price, if you pay less than $100, you're in the inexpensive range. You can get a good pair of binoculars for $200 to $300 and a great pair for $500. You can get a totally outstanding pair for $1,500 to $2,000.

ABOUT OPTICS: Optics involves a lot of science, stuff you may or may not want to know, but a couple of things are worth knowing by everyone who buys binoculars. The optics will be designated by two numbers, taking, as an example, the Brunton Externa Full-Size Binocular 8 x 45.

- *The power.* The first number (in the previous example it's the 8) tells you the power. What you see will be enlarged eight times. Powers over 10 won't work well without a tripod for stability. At more than 10 power, what you see will jiggle from the natural tremor of your hands.
- *The diameter of the lens.* The second number (45 in the previous example) tells you the diameter of the objective lens in millimeters. The objective lenses are the ones at the fronts of binoculars, the ones closest to what you're looking at, the ones that let in light. The larger the diameter, the more light an objective lens lets in and the better the image through the glass.

Photography

A packet of photos, more than anything else, will allow you to relive your camping adventures over and over. They'll show you not only where you went but also what

Want to capture it all on film? Join the crowd.

you did there. The candid, laughing, grubby faces around the campfire and on the trail will warm hearts forever. Take a camera.

If you're "serious" about taking photographs, be ready to spend from several hundred to several thousand dollars for the gear. With relatively expensive digital equipment, for example, you can produce professional-quality photographs with very little training. You, of course, don't have to be serious. Snapshots with very inexpensive cameras, including disposable cameras, may be all you'll ever want, capturing family and friends in the act of camping.

ON YOUR OWN

After you, your family, and perhaps your friends are comfortable camping in established campgrounds, the day may come when you want to strike out on your own. There's more work to do—finding a campsite, preparing a tent site, creating your own bathroom, leaving no trace when you head home. The rewards include a deep and pleasant sense of truly "going wild," the seclusion and privacy, and the satisfaction of increased self-reliance. In short, it can be a lot more fun. This chapter will give you a nudge toward camping on your own. This chapter may also remind you of information covered in previous chapters, and it is presented here again in the context of camping outside an established campground.

{ In the Words of a Sage }

We make ourselves rich by making our wants few.
—Henry David Thoreau

Choosing a Site

Do not wait until late in the day to select a campsite. You need plenty of time and light to set a proper camp. If you can't see, you can't do. Besides, you'll want to have camp set in time to enjoy a relaxing evening. If a site looks like a place for you, get out of your vehicle and take a good look around before unloading. Here's an old camping adage worth remembering: great campsites are found, not made.

"On your own" means there's no campground.

Safety First

You want, foremost, a site free of threats to the well-being of yourself and those with you. Threats may arise from several sources, including weather, overhanging dead limbs, or steep cliffs above or below your campsite.

Rain

Just because rain isn't predicted, doesn't mean it won't fall. If you see evidence that rain has puddled in or run through your choice of campsites, choose another site with more elevation. You especially need to avoid narrow canyons that could pose the risk of a flash flood in a downpour.

The best tent sites will be on sand, pea-sized gravel, or deep forest debris such as pine needles and leaves. These sites drain well if rain falls—and they're more comfortable to sleep on. Hard, compressed soil and ground already soggy will not drain well.

MORE ABOUT SAFETY:

TIP

- Do not set camp in the open or on ridges where you could be a primary lightning target, or near tall trees where you could be a secondary target.
- Do not set your camp underneath dead limbs still attached to trees or underneath dead trees—they could fall down in a high wind. Healthy trees, however, will provide wonderful shade on a hot day.
- Do not set camp near the edge of cliffs that someone might stumble off or at the bottom of cliffs that rocks could tumble off.

Wind

Wind can be a blessing and a curse. Breezes can drive away obnoxious insects, adding much to the serenity of a tent site. Gusty winds can keep you awake by "rattling the walls" and threatening to turn your tent or tarp into a kite. If wind poses a problem, choose a site behind natural windbreaks: a thick stand of trees, large rocks, a rise in the ground. Pitch your tent with the low end toward the wind, and pitch it as tightly as possible. Good tents will have sewn-on loops allowing you to add taut lines for more stability.

Cold

If it feels like a chilly night lies ahead, choose a site that is high rather than low. Cold air sinks, keeping the upper end of a valley slightly warmer than the lower end. Select a site, if you can, that will catch the early morning sun. First light striking your tent will add joy to your rising, as well as warmth on a cold morning.

THE HAPPY CAMPSITE:

TIP

- Make sure there's plenty of space for your vehicle, tent or tents, kitchen, and perhaps an acceptable fire site.
- Check for a nearby source of water—unless you're carrying plenty with you. If a natural source of water appears stagnant, however, consider camping somewhere else. Stagnant pools are often breeding sites for biting insects.
- Set your tent and your kitchen at least 200 feet, about seventy adult paces, from springs, streams, rivers, ponds, and lakes. Preventing human pollution from getting into natural water sources should rank high on your priority list.
- You're probably anticipating a fire, so check for an ample supply of dry wood. The firewood waiting to be gathered at a great campsite should be dead and on the ground. Breaking or sawing limbs from trees creates ugly scars that you don't want to leave behind.

DEFINING TERMS

Widowmakers are large, dead limbs, or even standing dead trees, that could fall on you or your tent.

- The fire site should be well away from the tent site, and upwind if you can determine the direction of prevailing winds. A flying ember will immediately melt through a tent wall or fly.
- Before building that fire, be certain that the fire danger is "low" and no fire ban is in effect. See "The Acceptable Fire" later in this chapter for more on camp fire restrictions.
- If you have to move obstacles out of the way, such as rocks or logs, replace them when you head home. You want to leave the site as you found it, or even in better shape than you found it (see Appendix A).

Good Water Versus Bad Water

Even if you've packed what you think will be enough water, it's best to have available some means to disinfect more—just in case you run out, or a herd of elk tramples the water carrier. Gone are the days when you could throw yourself down on your belly, tired and thirsty, and slurp up water from a crystalline-looking stream. It might be good—and it might be bad. And the only safe bet is to disinfect all wilderness water before drinking.

TECHNO: WATER DISINFECTION

- *Boiling water.* With enough fuel, you can *boil* water. In fact, by the time water has reached the boiling point, even at high altitudes, the organisms that cause disease are dead. The water does not have to roll around like a sea in a perfect storm to be safe to drink. The downside is that you use fuel and you have to wait for the water to cool to enjoy it.
- *Filtering water.* You may choose to pack a water filter. Some filters strain out only protozoa, such as *Giardia* and *Cryptosporidium.* A filter with a pore size of 1 micron or less will remove all protozoa. Some water filters remove protozoa and bacteria, but to do that they must have a pore size of 0.2 to 0.3 micron. Many types of filters are available, usually in outdoor specialty stores, that are capable of removing bacteria. No filters remove all viruses—they're simply too tiny. If you choose a water filter, be sure to read the label carefully to understand exactly what your filter will do for you. *And be warned:* all filters will eventually clog. Get a feel for your chosen filter—and when it reaches a point where you have to force water through it, you'll probably be forcing potentially dangerous microorganisms through as well. It's then time to change (or clean, as with ceramic filters) the filtering element.
- *Halogenating water.* Halogens are chemicals that are very good at killing everything harmful in water. Iodine and chlorine are the safest and most effective, but

no chemical guarantees water safe from *Cryptosporidium,* a very tough protozoa. A halogen can be added to water after filtering with a filter that removes only protozoa to guarantee safe water—and that's usually your safest bet. In most cases, iodine is the preferred chemical because it stores better and reacts less with organic compounds in water. Iodine is commercially available in several forms, the most popular being Potable Aqua tablets from the Wisconsin Pharmacal Company. The downside of iodine is the unappealing taste left in the water. You can rid the water of the iodine taste easily. Potable Aqua, for example, offers PA Plus, a harmless ascorbic acid tablet that removes all taint of iodine. You can also add any powdered drink mix to the water to override the iodine taste. It is critically important, however, that you add PA Plus or a drink mix only *after* the iodine has had sufficient time to kill the germs, usually thirty minutes. In every instance, carefully read the packaging of the product you use.

PRE-FILTERING WATER: Some wilderness water sources are awash with visible sediment or other debris. You'll get more and better use of your chosen water disinfection technique if you pre-filter such water. Before using a disinfection technique, pour the water through a bandanna or tee shirt—or better yet through a paper coffee filter—and into a bucket or large pot. Now you can disinfect the water from the bucket or pot with greater efficiency.

TIP

A filter, used properly, will almost always give you safe drinking water.

The Kitchen Area

Set up your camp kitchen near the fire—if you have one—but off to one side and out of traffic patterns. You don't want campers walking through the kitchen as they pass back and forth to the vehicle and the tent. If you have a camp table, set your stove on it to make cooking easier. If you have no table, you can use the tailgate of some vehicles. With no tailgate or table, you're left using a flat spot on the ground.

When choosing a kitchen area, pick a spot that will endure the trampling that kitchens always involve. There'll be plenty of standing and walking around, the kind of abuse that leaves a lasting impact. If the kitchen is sand or gravel, that'll be great. It should at least be free of vegetation that trampling will destroy, such as woody plants and flowers.

The Campfire

Without campground regulations to guide you, you must build a campfire that will cause the least impact on the environment.

- If previous campers left a fire ring, use it. Don't create another fire site.
- If no fire site already exists, choose a site that will leave the least impact. You can scoop out a shallow depression in sand or gravel, or you can dig a shallow pit for a fire in sandy, rocky, or gravely ground that has no overlying vegetation, no underlying roots, and no nearby dry grasses. Even if you are well away from a tree, you may still find yourself under overhanging branches, and you should not build a fire there. The heat may rise high enough to scorch or even kill the branches or start a fire in the tree.
- For the least impact, carry a fire pan, which can be anything metal: commercial fire pans, oil pans, aluminum roasting pans, garbage can lids. The pan must have sides high enough—3 inches will be enough—to contain the fire. Place the pan on a durable surface, such as gravel or sand, that will not be harmed by the fire. If you can't find a suitable surface, elevate the pan on a few rocks to prevent damage to the vegetation and soil that lie below. Fill the pan with a couple of inches of soil that contains no dead plant matter prior to building your fire.

Fire pan

1. The fire danger must be "low". You often will see signs on access roads telling you the fire danger. You can also check with land managers.
2. There must be no restrictions on the use of fires. Check with land management agencies to be sure. Land managers will also be able to tell you if there are specific regulations governing the use of fires.
3. Winds must be low. Even when the danger is low, high winds will cast sparks over alarming distances, and that should tell you "No fire."

BEDTIME FOR THE FIRE: Most often when you're on your own, you'll want the fire to die before you retire for the night. There also may be times when you'll want to awake to hot coals and brief work to get the fire going again. You can build up a bed of hot coals and "bank" them for the night by banking them into a mound. A well-banked bed of coals will often burn eight hours or more. Soon after rising, spread the mound to find the heat, add tinder and kindling, and soon a fresh fire blazes.

A SCATTERING OF ASHES: Be sure the ashes of your fire are completely drowned to death with water when you're breaking camp. You can scatter the drowned ash broadly without harming the environment. Do *not* just bury the ash. It'll eventually work its way to the surface in a clump. Ash in a clump will prevent plant growth while widely scattered ash breaks down quickly and adds nutrients to the soil.

The Outdoor Bathroom

Without the convenience of a campground's rest room, or even an outhouse, you're left with a problem: how to dispose of human fecal matter, which is not only unsightly and smelly but also full of germs. Improper handling of fecal matter can destroy an otherwise wonderful campsite, making it unappealing at best and somewhat dangerous at worst. You must manage disposal of human waste properly.

Portable Toilets

The simplest method for establishing an outdoor bathroom is to carry a portable toilet. Once again, you will have numerous choices, and you can spend well over $100 for a really nice portable toilet. Less expensive products are available, which will set you back only about $20, but they can be a bit tippy.

USING PORTABLE TOILETS:

- Set the toilet far enough *away from camp* to create privacy and to reduce the chance that insects will be attracted to your camp site.
- Increase privacy by hanging *a small tarp* as a shield.
- Buy and use any *chemicals* for your toilet that reduce the odor and increase the rate of decomposition of fecal matter.
- The toilet will, of course, have to be *cleaned after each trip,* a job that appeals to no one.

Cat Holes

Some campers opt for cat holes. For a cat hole, you'll need a small shovel or trowel. Dig at least 200 yards, about seventy adult paces, from any trail, road, or—most importantly—source of water to prevent contamination of the area. Dig down 6 to 8 inches, and make the hole about 4 to 6 inches wide. After using the cat hole, fill it in with the loose soil you dug out, and disguise the area with natural materials.

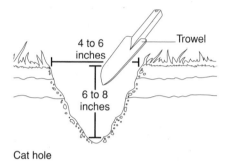

Cat hole

Latrines

A latrine is the least desirable option—partly because it requires more work and partly because it's more abusive to the environment. You might, however, choose a latrine if you plan to stay more than two or three nights in the same spot, and especially if you have small children along. Once again, dig at least 200 yards, about seventy adult paces, from any trail, road, or—most importantly—source of water. A latrine should be dug at least a foot deep and wider than it is deep. You'll need the soil you dug out to cover fecal matter immediately after each use. When a latrine is filled to within 4 inches of the top, it's time to stop using it and to fill in the rest of the space with soil, once again disguising the spot with natural material.

Just the Facts: The Half-Life of Toilet Paper

Toilet paper must *not* be buried. Despite opinions to the contrary, it will not decompose for a very long time. Toilet paper can be thrown into a portable toilet or garbage bag, or it can be burned in a fire.

Camp Showers

There's nothing quite like a hot shower, and you don't need to deny yourself the pleasure when camping. Not that there's anything wrong with being dirty for awhile—as long as you wash your hands after defecating and before preparing food. It's just that a shower feels good.

Several solar showers are available on the market. Essentially they're plastic bags you fill with water and place in direct sunlight until the water heats. On a bright day, they can produce amazingly hot water. Hang one from a tree limb, stand beneath it, and open the valve. You won't have enough water for a prolonged wash, but you can get squeaky and happily clean. If you use soap, remember to take your shower at least 200 yards from any natural water sources.

AN IMPROVISED SHOWER: For a quick warm rinse on a sunny day, carry a one-gallon plastic jug that you've painted black. Poke a few holes in the lid. In direct sunlight, the water will heat up nicely.

Breaking Camp Redux

Camp break-down has been discussed (see Chapter 4), but remember to hide evidence of your on-your-own camp:

- Gather every scrap of litter, even food scraps.
- Replace rocks and logs, even large limbs, you may have moved.
- Cover scuffed up areas with pine needles, leaves, or forest debris.
- Fluff up matted grass.
- Do anything else you can think to do that makes the site look unused.

It might be hard to say goodbye.

11

COMING HOME

Coming home typically stirs up mixed feelings. It was great to be out there, and it's great to be back on familiar ground. Check the mail, answer your phone messages, and take a long, hot shower. Before too long you'll want to drop off the photos to be developed and read through your journal, reminding yourself of your experiences and what you learned. If you haven't already, you'll soon be making plans for your next camping trip.

But don't get too comfortable. Your camping gear must be properly cleaned and stored for the next journey, steps that will not only keep your gear ready to go but also prolong its life expectancy.

{ In the Words of a Sage }

We go to sanctuaries to remember the things we hold most dear, the things we cherish and love. And then—our greatest challenge—we return home seeking to enact this wisdom as best we can in our daily lives.
—*William Cronan*

Cleaning: The Tent
Storing a tent clean, dry, and ready for your next adventure will add years to its usefulness and a pleasant start to future trips.

- If you're not sure the tent was clean and completely dry before you packed it, set it up in the yard.

- Shake out or wipe out dirt and debris.
- If the dirt is ground in, use a damp sponge and, if needed, a mild soap such as hand soap that comes in one of those pump bottles. Detergents and bleach are forbidden since they can damage the fabric and the waterproof coating.
- Be sure to rinse off all soap residue.
- Be sure the zippers are clean. Dirt embedded in zippers shortens zipper life.
- Zippers that have failed may be fixable, or they may have to be replaced, jobs that can be done quickly by specialty shops.
- Wipe clean the tent poles and stakes before storing them.
- If the tent leaked at all, seal the seams again.
- Check for damage. Patch tears and holes. You can patch with duct tape or, for a longer-lasting job, with urethane adhesive patches. In both cases, the material you patch with must be applied to a clean, dry surface. Wiping around the tear with alcohol will clean the surface well, and alcohol dries quickly.
- When the tent is clean, dry, and prepped for the next trip, store it loose. Don't cram it into a stuff sack until you're packing your vehicle.

TIP

PATCHING HOLES: If the patching material you use to patch any holes or tears has corners, cut them round. Square corners peel up easily while rounded corners will stay flat for many trips.

{ Personal Reflections }

I had some tents for many years, and I can't set one up without a flood of fond memories. They seem to stick to the nylon like the tangy smell of wood smoke. And my tents have never failed me in any way. Why? Because (a) they're high-quality products, and (b) I've taken very good care of them—as I try to do with all my friends.

Cleaning: The Bedroom
You don't want to climb into a dirty bed at home. Why do it on your next trip?

- *Sleeping pads.* Store your sleeping pads after they are clean and dry. As with tents, you can wash pads with a sponge and mild soap, rinsing off any soap residue. If your pad is an air mattress, you can store it rolled loosely. If you have a self-inflating pad, store it unrolled with the valve open. The foam will last longer if kept uncrushed, and the open valve will allow moisture that got inside to escape.
- *Sleeping bags.* Sleeping bags always benefit from some airing time, inside out, before storage. They can endure a lot of use between washings. If they're soiled, however, follow carefully the specific directions for washing that came with the bag. Bags will last longer if you keep them relatively clean and store them loose. If the insulation is kept compressed, it loses its loft. Stuff bags into their small sacks just before packing your vehicle.

STORING SLEEPING BAGS: If your sleeping bag came with a large storage bag, use it. If it didn't, you can store it separately in a large, cotton laundry bag.

STORING OTHER GEAR:

- *Do not store anything wet.* Mildew will compromise the integrity of anything.
- *Do not dry for very long or store anything synthetic in direct sunlight.* Ultraviolet light deteriorates most artificial fibers.
- *Do not store anything dirty.* Scrub the pots and pans. Wash the clothes. Use a damp sponge to wipe out the tent and pack. Clean and oil the leather boots.
- *Do not put off making repairs,* sealing seams, replacing what needs replacing, and righting wrongs.

Cleaning: The Kitchen

Your stove will not only last longer but will function better if you keep it clean. Your other kitchen gear should be stored germ free and ready for use, just like at home.

- *The stove.* Most stoves come with cleaning instructions and often with repair instructions. Compressed air in cans, which you can find at computer stores for cleaning a keyboard, can be used to blow off debris from hard-to-reach spots. For rubber rings at connection points, such as where a fuel tank attaches to a stove, keep the rubber moist—lip balm will work for that. If the rubber parts have dried out and cracked, replace them. Store the stove clean and prepped for your next trip. Do not store fuel inside a stove's fuel tank. Old fuel will break down and form impurities that will clog the stove the next time you fire it up.
- *The kitchenware.* Even if you washed your kitchenware before breaking down camp, the pots, pans, and other gear may not be quite as clean as everything appeared in camp. Take a look, and clean the stuff that needs it before storing. Store knives not only clean but also sharpened.
- *The cooler.* After washing out the cooler, give it some open-air time to get rid of odors before you store it. If odors persist in the cooler, you can eliminate them by wiping the inside with lemon juice or bleach.

Cleaning: The Closet

Store your outdoor clothing clean and ready to pack—or clean and packed if you want to be ready to hit the road fast. Follow carefully the washing directions on the labels of synthetic clothing. Patch anything that needs patching, and seal the seams on raingear if it leaked. Don't store your footwear cloaked in dirt, mud, or debris. If you use leather boots, give them a good brushing and a quick coat of boot oil. When you're sure your footwear is dry, store boots and shoes in a well-ventilated area.

Cleaning: Bits and Pieces

Every piece of equipment deserves a check before storage. Take care of your gear, and it will take care of you.

- Camp tables and chairs are safely stored folded after they're clean and dry.
- Go through your first-aid kit, replacing items you used, materials damaged by water, and medications that have reached their expiration dates.
- Store the lantern clean and empty of fuel if it uses a liquid fuel.
- Store your flashlights clean and dry. Store your batteries outside your flashlight to make sure they also are dry.
- Clean the saw, hatchet, and shovel, and store them dry. Hone the hatchet's edge a bit if you used it.
- Replace items you used from the repair kit.

APPENDIX A

LEAVE NO TRACE

With the growth in its popularity, camping has been hard on the land—not camping in general, but camping without a sense of responsibility to protect our natural resources. As little as 150 years ago, it was a tough job surviving in wild country. Now wild country is having a tough time surviving all the people who love camping. Some camping areas have even been closed due to overuse and abuse. Problems often arise from the fact that campers don't know how to use the land without abusing it. This is especially true if you camp on your own, outside an established campground (see Chapter 10). For that reason, the National Outdoor Leadership School (NOLS) and the four federal land management agencies—National Park Service, U.S. Forest Service, Bureau of Land Management, U.S. Fish & Wildlife Service—created the principles of a program called "Leave No Trace." The program is managed by NOLS and The Leave No Trace Center for Outdoor Ethics (see Appendix E). The purpose of the Leave No Trace program is to educate campers and other wildland users to reduce human impact to nothing—or at least to a bare minimum.

Leave No Trace Principles
1. Plan ahead and prepare.
2. Travel and camp on durable surfaces.

3. Dispose of waste properly.
4. Leave what you find.
5. Minimize campfire impacts.
6. Respect wildlife.
7. Be considerate of other visitors.

Plan Ahead

You can take steps before you leave home to reduce the chance you'll leave a trace. You can, for example, reduce the amount of garbage you carry by repackaging food and getting rid of trash you might leave behind accidentally. You can, and should, go prepared to deal with extremes of weather and any emergencies that might arise to minimize your use of the area's resources. You should go knowledgeable of any regulations or special concerns for the area you'll visit.

Most importantly, you can learn about the environment you intend to camp in, and how to minimize your impact on that particular environment. Deserts, for example, can be harmed in ways that differ from high mountains and seashores.

TIP

REDUCING TRASH:

- Take granola bars out of their boxes and their wrappers and carry them in one zip-top plastic bag.
- Pour individual packets of instant oatmeal into one zip-top bag.
- Instead of carrying multiple boxes of different types of tea bags, carry them all in one zip-top bag.

Travel and Camp on Durable Surfaces

Litter is ugly but easily picked up. Trampled vegetation and eroded trails, under the other foot, might last for years—or a lifetime. Choose to set your feet and/or your tent on surfaces that endure: rock, sand, gravel, dry grasses, sedges, and snow.

In popular areas, concentrate your use where it is obvious other visitors have already left an impact. Stay on trails, avoid shortcuts, use campsites and fire rings that others have used. And leave your campsite as clean and natural as possible.

In pristine areas without noticeable impact, disperse your use. When you travel off-trail, walk on durable surfaces and avoid creating obvious campsites. Groups should not walk in single file off-trail, trampling the earth into a visible pathway. Spend no more than one night at a pristine site.

Dispose of Waste Properly

Always carry trash bags, and keep one handy. Inspect your campsites and your rest spots, and leave nothing behind, even micro-trash. Pack out leftover food, as well as your trash. And lend a hand by packing out the refuse discarded by others.

Human Waste

Dispose of your human waste thoughtfully and appropriately. Use outhouses and rest rooms if they are there. Consider carrying a portable toilet (see Chapter 10). Otherwise dig a cat hole 6 to 8 inches deep at least 200 feet (about seventy adult steps) from water, camp, trails, and drainages. When you've finished using a cat hole, fill it in and disguise the site. If you choose to use toilet paper, pack it out or burn it in your campfire. Urinate away from camps and trails on rocks or bare ground rather than on vegetation. Where water is plentiful, consider diluting the urine by rinsing the site.

Dish Washing

To wash your dishes and cookware, carry water 200 feet away from streams or lakes. Strain dirty dish water with a fine-mesh strainer (or an old nylon stocking) before scattering the dirty water. Pack out the material left in the strainer. Soap, even biodegradable soap, can affect the water quality of lakes and streams, so use it minimally.

Body Washing

Always wash yourself at least 200 feet from shorelines, and rinse with water carried in a pot. Consider using a hand sanitizer that allows you to wash your hands without worrying about waste-water disposal.

TEACH YOUR CHILDREN WELL: Make a game out of finding and removing everything left behind by you or other campers—and tell your children why you're doing it.

Leave What You Find

Sometimes what you do *not* see creates the most disturbing impact of camping. Archaeological and historical artifacts are reminders of the rich human history of North America, and they belong to all people for all time. Structures, dwellings, and artifacts on public lands are protected by the Archaeological Resources Protection Act and the National Historic Preservation Act, and they should not be disturbed. Do not pick the flowers, collect the rocks, or take the deer antlers home to decorate your office wall. If you want a souvenir, take a photo, draw a picture, and cherish the memories.

Minimize Campfire Impacts

The lasting impacts of traditional open fires can be avoided by using lightweight stoves. If fires are acceptable, build a small, minimum-impact fire, using an existing fire ring or a fire pan you brought with you (see Chapter 10). Use only dead and downed wood—nothing bigger around than your wrist. Keep the fire small, burn all the wood down to ash, saturate the ash with water, and scatter the ash broadly. Be sure to pick and pack out any garbage you dropped in the fire that failed to fully burn. If you used an existing fire ring, leave it for the next camper, but get rid of all evidence of *your* fire. If more than one fire ring exists, consider dismantling unnecessary rings and hiding the evidence that more than one existed.

Respect Wildlife

Although some wild animals adapt to human presence, others flee, sometimes abandoning their young and their preferred habitat. Observe quietly from a distance. Avoid quick movements and direct eye contact, actions that may be interpreted as aggression. And do not, intentionally or unintentionally—by leaving trash or storing food unsecured—feed wildlife. If you must travel with your pet, make sure that local regulations allow it, and control your pet at all times.

Be Considerate of Other Visitors

Yes, you're an owner of public land, along with millions of others. And they, too, deserve respect. The little things are often the most important. Simple courtesies—such as offering a friendly greeting to other campers, stepping aside to let someone pass you on a trail, waiting patiently for a turn, or preserving the quiet—all make a difference. Practice trail etiquette. Hikers should move to the downhill side and talk quietly to horseback riders as they pass. Before passing others, politely announce your presence and proceed with caution. Lend a hand, if appropriate, to help those ahead. Take rest breaks a short distance (and out of sight when possible) from the trail on durable surfaces. If possible, camp out of sight and sound of trails and other visitors.

APPENDIX B

BEST OF THE BEST CAMPGROUNDS

Experience being an excellent—though sometimes unkind—teacher, it would be mighty helpful if you could tap into the experiences of long-time campers from across the nation to harvest their opinions about the best campgrounds. They have, after all, been there and done it. Well, you can!

The Top 100 Family Campgrounds

ReserveAmerica stands out as a campground reservation service, offering access to almost 3000 parks and more than 150,000 campsites. More than that, this organization collected information and opinions from park managers, park rangers, and campers themselves to create a list of the top family campgrounds. The 100 best for 2005 were chosen based on criteria that included overall beauty, access to activities (family beaches, hiking trails, visitor centers, educational programs, children's events), radio-free (quiet) zones, and park amenities (water, rest rooms, hot showers, laundry rooms)—plus all the finalists are located within 100 miles of a metropolitan area. Go to www.reserveamerica.com for a wealth of information and to make a reservation.

California

Big Basin Redwoods State Park: a mixture of lush canyons, brushy slopes, and wildlife.

Brannan Island State Recreation Area: countless islands and wildlife-rich marshes.

Del Norte Coast Redwoods State Park: old-growth forest and eight miles of wild coastline.

Humboldt Redwoods State Park: magnificent groves of old-growth redwoods.

Mackerricher State Park: a variety of beach, dunes, forest, and wetlands.

Malakoff Diggins State Historic Park: huge cliffs carved by mighty streams.

Manzanita Lake Campground: the best of Lassen Volcanic National Park.

Mount Diablo State Park: see thirty-five of California's fifty-eight counties from the top.

Patrick's Point State Park: high cliffs overlooking a spectacular coastline.

Pfeiffer Big Sur State Park: an outstanding forest and wide open meadows.

Salt Point State Park: six miles of the Sonoma Coast with sandy beaches and tall cliffs.

Colorado

Colorado River State Park: great scenery near Grand Mesa.

Golden Gate Canyon State Park: mountain splendor just west of Denver.

Mueller State Park: aspen and conifer forests rich with wildlife.

Ridgway State Recreation Area: a lovely reservoir beneath towering mountains.

Steamboat Lake State Park: absolutely breathtaking scenery.

Connecticut

American Legion State Forests: lovely forests divided by a wild and scenic river.

Housatonic Meadows State Park: the picturesque valley of the Housatonic River.

Macedonia Brook State Park: springs, streams, and outstanding views of the Catskills.

Mashamoquet Brook State Park: a woodland paradise.

Rocky Neck State Park: a half mile of crescent-shaped, sandy beach.

Florida

Alexander Springs Recreation Area: beautiful springs and abundant wildlife.

Bahia Honda State Park: one of the best beaches in south Florida.

Georgia

Petersburg Campground: on lovely Thurmond Lake, and not far from Augusta.

Idaho

Dent Acres Campground: in Idaho's beautiful Clearwater Valley.

Dworshak State Park: shady trees and bright meadows on the shore of a reservoir.

Farragut State Park: on the shore of Idaho's largest lake.
Hells Gate State Park: the deepest river gorge in North America.
Ponderosa State Park: on Payette Lake and the edge of the Salmon River Mountains.
Priest Lake State Park: nestled below the crest of the Selkirk Mountains.

Illinois

Lithia Springs Recreation Area: on Lake Shelbyville, with a wealth of fish
   and wildlife.
South Sandusky Campground: on Rend Lake in the heart of southern Illinois.

Iowa

Prairie Flower Recreation Area: wide open land and a lovely lake.

Kentucky

Baileys Point Campground: waterfront campsites on Barren River Lake.
Kendall Campground: on Lake Cumberland, and near a fish hatchery.

Massachusetts

Clarksburg State Park: breathtaking views of the Berkshires and Green Mountains.
D. A. R. State Forest: on a ridge between Highland Lake and scenic wetlands.
Mohawk Trail State Forest: a cold, clear river cascading through a quiet forest.
Nickerson State Park: a natural woodland in the heart of Cape Cod.
Otter River State Forest: a beautiful pine forest on Beaman Pond.
Pearl Hill State Park: large, private sites beneath stately pines.
Salisbury Beach State Reservation: Almost four miles of Atlantic Ocean beach.
Scusset Beach State Reservation: a beach on Cape Cod Bay.
Tolland State Forest: on a scenic peninsula into Otis Reservoir.
Wells State Park: a woodland in central Massachusetts.

Michigan

Brevort Lake Campground: a dense forest on a lovely lake.

Missouri

Greenville Recreation Area: on Wappapello Lake in the splendid Ozark Mountains.

Nevada

Nevada Beach Campground: on simply outstanding Lake Tahoe.

New York

Cranberry Lake Campground: one of the largest remote areas left in New York.
Glimmerglass State Park: wooded sites and a beach on Ostego Lake.

Heckscher State Park: shady sites on Long Island.
Lake Erie State Park: wooded sites near the shore of Lake Erie.
Lake Harris Campground: forested sites stretched along the shore of a large lake.
Lakeside Beach State Park: a forested area on the shore of Lake Ontario.
Lake Taghkanic State Park: a beach and a forest on a splendid little body of water.
Lewey Lake Campground: a splendid forest in Adirondack Park.
Long Point State Park: a long, lean peninsula reaching out into the water of the Finger Lakes.
Meacham Lake Campground: wooded sites on a quiet lake.
Moreau Lake State Park: a beautiful forest on a lovely lake.
North–South Lake Campground: scenic twin lakes on the eastern edge of the Catskills.
Watkins Glen State Park: an excellent forest near the shore of Seneca Lake.

North Carolina
Linville Falls Campground: near the Linville River, just off the Blue Ridge Parkway.

Oregon
Diamond Lake Recreation Area: in the outstanding Umpqua National Forest.
LePage Park Recreation Area: a lovely basin near the meeting of two rivers.

Pennsylvania
Tub Run Recreation Area: forested mountains falling into Youghiogheny River Lake.

South Carolina
Calhoun Falls State Recreation Area: on Lake Russell, one of the state's most popular.
Devils Fork State Park: on Lake Jocassee in the lovely Blue Ridge Mountains.
Dreher Island State Recreation Area: three beautiful islands in Lake Murray.
Hamilton Branch State Recreation Area: in the Piedmont area, and on Thurmond Lake.
Kings Mountain State Park: a picturesque setting with two small lakes.
Lake Greenwood State Recreation Area: forested sites on a beautiful lake.
Lake Hartwell State Recreation Area: fourteen miles of outstanding shoreline.
Myrtle Beach State Park: one of the most popular of South Carolina's beaches.
Oconee State Park: on a wooded plateau in the foothills of the Blue Ridge Mountains.
Santee State Park: on Lake Marion in the legendary Santee–Cooper Country.
Twin Lakes Campground: a popular destination not far from Clemson.

Tennessee
Defeated Creek Park: on a peninsula into Cordell Hull Lake.

Texas
Chisos Basin Campground: in the rugged hills of Big Bend National Park.
Rio Grande Village Campground: raw splendor in Big Bend National Park.

Utah
Antelope Island State Park: the largest island in the Great Salt Lake.
Bear Lake State Park: nestled in the Rocky Mountains not far from Idaho.
Dead Horse Point State Park: standing 2000 vertical feet above the
 Colorado River.
Red Fleet State Park: majestic slickrock formations in northeastern Utah.
Wasatch Mountain State Park: in beautiful Heber Valley, with towering
 peaks nearby.
Willard Bay State Park: on the shore of the Great Salt Lake.

Vermont
Winhall Brook Campground: where two rivers meet in the Green Mountains.

Virginia
Chippokes Plantation State Park: a living exhibit of rural agriculture in America.
Douthat State Park: in the Allegheny Mountains, once named among America's
 ten best lesser-known parks.
Kiptopeke State Park: on Chesapeake Bay; a truly outstanding birding area.
North Bend Park: lovely wooded sites on Kerr Reservoir.
Pocahontas State Park: one of the state's most popular, and not far
 from Richmond.
Salthouse Branch Park: a pristine lake in mountainous terrain.

Washington
Chief Timothy Park: a beautiful private campground near Clarkston.

West Virginia
Gerald Freeman Campground: nestled in the headwaters of Sutton Lake.
Robert W. Craig Campground: a lovely lake set in rugged hills.

Wisconsin
Buckhorn State Park: a peninsula jutting into the Wisconsin River.
Devils Lake State Park: 500-foot bluffs tower over a 360-acre lake.
Kohler–Andrae State Park: a scenic gem on the shore of Lake Michigan.

Peninsula State Park: high bluffs, a cobblestone shoreline, and a sandy beach.

Roche-A-Cri State Park: a panoramic view of extensive prairie.

The Top 20 "Wild" Campgrounds

Backpacker Magazine went from sea to shining sea to compile a list of the twenty best campgrounds for those looking for a site a bit more off the beaten track. But don't let the "wild" fool you. You can still drive your vehicle to most of them, set up your tent at an improved site, and enjoy at least a few amenities. You'll also find some of the most splendid natural wonders right outside your tent window at these campgrounds. Go to *www.backpacker.com* for more information.

California

Jumbo Rocks Campground, Joshua Tree National Park: pit toilets, no water, cactus-filled desert valleys, and a magnificent jumble of jagged rocks (760-367-5500, *www.nps.gov/jotr*).

Manzanita Campground, Lassen Volcanic National Park: water, rest rooms, showers, a 10,457-foot peak, and a hotbed of geothermal activity (530-595-4444, *www.nps.gov/lavo*).

Selby Campground, Carrizo Plain National Monument: pit toilets, no water, an education center, and large birds soaring over extensive grasslands (661-391-6000, *http://ca.blm.gov/bakersfield/carrizoplain.html*).

Scorpion Valley Campground, Santa Cruz Island, Channel Islands National Park: a boat shuttle to pit toilets, water, dark canyons splitting rugged mountains, and sandy beaches (805-658-5730, *www.nps.gov/chis*).

The Northeast

Dry River Campground, Crawford Notch State Park, New Hampshire: rest rooms, water, showers, near the tallest peak and the highest waterfall in the state (603-374-2272, *www.nhparks.state.nh.us*).

Lake George Islands, Adirondack Park, New York: toilets, water, and forty-four islands to choose from, accessible only by boat on Lake George (518-656-9426, *www.dec.state.ny.us*).

Sperry Road Campground, Mount Greylock State Reservation, Massachusetts: pit toilets, water, the Berkshire Mountains, and near the summit of the state's highest peak (413-499-4262, *www.state.ma.us/dem/parks/mgry.htm*).

Warren Island State Park, Maine: pit toilets, water, an isolated island accessible only by sea kayak or canoe (207-941-4014, *www.state.me.us*).

The Northwest

Eagle Creek Campground, Columbia River Gorge National Scenic Area, Oregon: rest rooms, water, a quiet forest high above a massive river gorge

(541-308-1700, *www.fs.fed.us/r6/columbia/forest*).

Hidden Campground, Hells Canyon National Recreation Area, Oregon: vault toilets, no water, the Wallowa Mountains, and the wild and scenic Snake River (541-426-4978, *www.fs.fed.us/hellscanyon*).

Lower Falls Recreation Area, Mount Saint Helens National Volcanic Monument, Washington: rest rooms, water, showers, on the banks of the Lewis River near the devastation of the mighty 1980 eruption (360-449-7800, *www.fs.fed.us/gpnf*).

Mora Campground, Olympic National Park, Washington: rest rooms, water, old-growth forest, and the longest stretch of wilderness beach in the United States (360-374-5460, *www.nps.gov/olym*).

Rocky Mountains

Echo Park Campground, Dinosaur National Monument, Colorado: rest rooms, water, a dinosaur quarry, and a deep canyon where the Yampa and Green Rivers meet (970-374-3000, *www.nps.gov/dino*).

Kintla Lake Campground, Glacier National Park, Montana: vault toilets, no water, an alpine lake, and classic glacier-carved scenery (406-888-7800, *www.nps.gov/glac*).

Pinyon Flats Campground, Great Sand Dunes National Park, Colorado: rest rooms, water, and North America's tallest sand dunes near the Sangre de Cristo Mountains (719-378-6399, *www.nps.gov/grsa*).

Teton Campground, Caribou–Targhee National Forest, Wyoming: vault toilets, water, a babbling creek filled with trout near the Grand Tetons (208-524-7500, *www.fs.fed.us/r4/caribou-targhee*).

The South

Dog Canyon Campground, Guadalupe Mountains National Park, Texas: toilets, water, towering desert peaks near Carlsbad Caverns (915-828-3251, *www.nps.gov/gumo*).

Lava Point Campground, Zion National Park, Utah: toilets, no water, shaded sites on a dirt road in a slickrock mecca of orange magnificence (435-722-3256, *www.nps.gov/zion*).

Meriwether Lewis Monument Campground, Natchez Trace Parkway, Tennessee: rest rooms, water, a forested ridge overlooking a creek near the grave of Meriwether Lewis (800-305-7417, *www.nps.gov/natr*).

Sea Camp Campground, Cumberland Island National Seashore, Georgia: rest rooms, water, cold showers, shady live oaks near the ocean, and a huge island to explore (912-882-4336, *www.nps.gov/cuis*).

APPENDIX C

BOREDOM BUSTERS

Maybe it's the rain. Or maybe there was an early hatch of hordes of mosquitoes. Anyway, you are stuck in the tent—but it doesn't have to ruin the camping trip. You can bust the boredom! These ideas are written with a family in mind, but, hey, there's still a child somewhere inside all of us.

1. *Story Time.* Someone starts a story by making up the first line. Each family member adds a line, and the story grows as it's passed from person to person. "Once upon a time there was a. . . . "
2. *Story Time, Part II.* Take notes. You may be on hand for the birth of another Winnie-the-Pooh.
3. *Family Letter Writing.* You'll need a pen or pencil and paper. Write a family letter to Grandma and Grandpa, or somebody else special. Take turns thinking up the next line of the letter.
4. *Family Letter Writing, Part II.* Write a family letter to someone in a powerful position (the governor, the president of the United States). Tell that person what the family thinks about an important issue—such as environmental problems and concerns.

5. *Books.* Make sure everyone has packed a book. Coloring books work for the little people. A quiet hour of reading, and the weather may change in your favor.

6. *Books, Part II:* Carry a favorite family book, or one that could become a family favorite, and take turns reading aloud. The *Goosebumps* series has worked especially well for my family.

7. *Books, Part III.* Many books for young readers are rich with dialogue. Divide up the characters in the book. You'll need a narrator. Snuggle up around the book with each family member reading aloud the words of his or her character. If you get stuck with more than one character, change your voice to fit the characters.

8. *Natural Art.* Pack a tube of glue and several pieces of paper. Gather what you can reach from the tent door (small sticks, pine needles, leaves) and what "trash" you can find in your tent or pockets (gum wrappers, lint, pennies). Create a piece of family memorabilia by gluing the stuff to the paper in creative designs. Or, if you gather enough items, have everyone create their own designs.

9. *Pick-Up Twiggies.* Gather a handful of small twigs, as straight as possible, and use them to play the old game of Pick-Up Sticks. One child holds the handful of twigs and lets them drop into a tangled pile. If the initial player can pick up a twig without disturbing the rest of the pile, that player gets the twig and the chance to go again. It's okay to use a twig you've won to help pick up the next twig. Disturb another twig in the pile, and play passes to the next group member.

10. *Twig Writing.* Use the twigs from Pick-Up Twiggies, or any other twigs or pine needles, to form letters (for nonreaders) or words (for readers) on the floor of the tent.

11. *Twig Writing, Part II.* In this advanced form of Twig Writing, you can write a word with twigs and remove several of the twigs. The rest of the family has to figure out the word and replace the missing twigs.

12. *Twig Home Building.* Use twigs, and rocks and leaves, to construct miniature log homes inside the tent. Glue, if you've thought to pack it, can be useful. *Note: after this activity, you may find your sleeping bag stuck to your sleeping pad.*

13. *"Easter Egg" Hunt.* You'll need a handful of small rocks. While everyone hides their eyes, you hide the rocks around the inside of the tent (in, for example, pockets, sleeping bags, stuff sacks, unused socks). When you're ready, say "go" and see who finds the most "eggs." *Note: be ready for several minutes of turbulence.*

14. *"Easter Egg" Hunt, Part II.* Hide candy.

15. *"Easter Egg" Hunt, Part III.* Make it a timed event—three minutes and the game starts again.

16. *Caterpillar.* Everyone will have to have their sleeping bags handy. "It" closes

his or her eyes, and everybody else switches bags and scrunches down deep inside, like caterpillars in their cocoons. "It" has to figure out who's who by feeling through the bag.

17. *Checkers.* Prior to leaving home, use a permanent marker to draw a checkerboard on the bottom of a foamlite sleeping pad. Use rocks for one player and small sticks for the other.

18. *Doctor.* Open your first-aid kit and take turns being the "doctor." This game teaches kids how to properly use the items in the kit.

19. *Simon Says.* This old game works great in tents. One player starts as "Simon." "Simon" tells the rest of the family, "Simon says, do this," and then performs an action such as grabbing the right foot with the left hand or clapping hands. When Simon Says do something, everyone must do the action. If Simon says, "Do this," and performs an action without saying "Simon says," anyone who performs the action is out of the game. The idea is to get the game moving fast enough so the other players fail to notice that "Simon" did not say "Simon says."

20. *Map Reading.* You'll need a topographical map of the area and pencils and paper. Pencils that write in different colors are especially fun. After you've taught the kids how to read the map, pick a section and have everyone draw a picture of what that part of the map might look like in real life.

21. *Map Reading, Part II.* Lump a sleeping bag in the center of the tent, creating hills and valleys. Lay a blue tee shirt in for a lake, or stretch out a blue bandanna for a river. Now everyone can draw a "topographical map" of the sleeping bag.

22. *Slap Jacks.* A deck of cards offers virtually endless opportunities to end boredom in a tent. In Slap Jacks the deck is divided among the family members, and all players keep their cards face down in front of them. When the game leader says "go," players turn up their top card on the playing "field." The high card takes all the cards on the field. When a jack is turned, the first player to slap it gets all the cards on the field. When you run out of cards, you're relegated to watching the rest of the game. *Note: the deck may not endure a lot of games.*

23. *Whosker-Do.* In this card game your memory is tested. All the cards are laid face down and spread out in the middle of the tent. When it's your play, turn up any two cards. If they match, you get to keep them, and you get to go again. When all the cards are matched, the game ends.

24. *Old Maid.* Remove all but one queen from a deck of cards. She becomes the "Old Maid." Shuffle and deal the remaining cards until they've all been dealt. For smaller hands, you can use half a deck. Anyone with a "set" of all four aces, all four fours, etc., matches them and lays them down. With half a deck, of course, you only need both aces, etc. The player to your left then picks one card from your hand. If it makes a set, that player lays down the set and picks again. Who'll end up being the Old Maid?

25. *Crazy Eights.* Each player is dealt eight cards from a regular deck. The play starts when the dealer places one card from his or her hand face up in the middle of the tent. The player to the left must play a card that (1) matches the suit or (2) matches the value of the card (a four can play another four, a king another king, despite the suit, etc.). If, say, a five of diamonds is played on a five of hearts, the suit changes to diamonds. If the next player cannot play, he or she draws a card from the remainder of the deck. The eights are "crazy." They can be played anytime. They can be any suit, any value. The choice belongs to whoever plays an eight. Who'll empty their hand of cards first?

26. *In the Pot.* Put one of the cooking pots on one side of the tent while everyone else crowds over to the other side. Take turns with a pile of small rocks or twigs or pinecones to see who can toss the most into the pot. Keep track, and see who can get to ten or a hundred first.

27. *In the Pot, Part II.* Place several containers (pots, cups, bowls) across the tent. Place values on the containers determined by the difficulty of tossing a rock or pine cone inside. The large pot, for example, scores one, and the cup scores five.

28. *In the Pot, Part III.* In this advanced form of *In the Pot,* you lay a twig across and perpendicular to another twig. Hit the end of the top twig so that it flies through the air. Aim for the pot.

29. *In the Pot, Part IV.* If you have a deck of cards, try throwing them, one at a time, into the pot. You can score the game by taking turns and counting the value of the cards (face cards score ten, an ace scores one, a five scores five, etc.).

30. *Basket Weaving.* You'll need long stems of grass. Lay a dozen stems flat on the tent floor. Weave another dozen, over and under, perpendicular to the first dozen, and tighten up the weaving so that you end up with a square with twelve stems sticking out in all four directions. Turn up the loose ends to form the sides and weave more grass in and out until the sides are complete. Turn down the tops of the stems left sticking up, and weave them into the sides. Voilà! A small basket.

31. *Touch, but Don't Look.* Take a stuff sack, or a paper bag, and secretly put in lots of different things (pinecone, spoon, flower, rock, stick, etc.). Without looking, your child must stick his or her hand in the sack, pick up an object, and decide what it is before pulling it out. Let the child have a turn filling the bag, and you do the guessing—if you dare stick in your hand.

32. *Micro-Exploration.* You'll need a magnifying glass. Sometimes you'll find one as a part of your compass. Spend time closely examining common things around the tent and camp: the weave of cloth, a bug's legs and antennae, the composition of a leaf, the surface of a rock, human skin. There's a whole new world waiting to be explored.

33. *Storytelling.* Just about everybody enjoys a good tale well told. Read up beforehand. Books of "campfire tales" abound. Ghost stories seem especially

appropriate. It may be, after all, dark and stormy outside.

34. *Twenty Questions.* In this old game one player starts by saying "I'm thinking of a famous person" or "I'm thinking of a famous place." What he or she is thinking of doesn't matter, as long as it's famous. Then the other players get to ask questions until the riddle is solved. *Note: don't bother trying to keep track of the number of questions.*

35. *I Spy.* This is another old game in which one players says, " I spy . . . ," finishing the sentence with a partial description of some object in sight: "I spy something brown." "I spy something hanging from a tree." Add more descriptors until the object is "spied" by someone else. That person gets to be the "spy-er." Keep it simple for younger kids. Add complexity for older kids: "I spy something with a big mouth" (answer: a water bottle).

36. *I Went to the Woods.* This game involves the alphabet and creative thinking. The game leader says, "I went to the woods and found an *a*(nt)." The next person says "I went to the woods and found a *b*(all)." And so it goes through the alphabet. For older kids, add complexity by limiting what you can find. For example, you can find only animals, or you can find only food.

37. *I Went to the Woods, Part II.* In this more advanced game, you can find anything in the woods, but the next player has to *add* his or her "thing" to the list. "I went to the woods and found an umbrella." Next: "I went to the woods and found an umbrella and a hat." Next: "I went to the woods and found an umbrella and a hat and a dog." Etc.

38. *Memory Game.* You'll need to gather sets of similar materials for each player. What you gather doesn't matter: a rock, a couple of twigs, a spoon, a match, stems of grass, a dandelion. While everyone closes their eyes, you arrange your materials on the tent floor in a unique design. When you're ready, say "Go," and the other players study the design for several seconds. Then cover your design with a shirt or bandanna. The other players now have to re-create your design from memory with their materials. The closest re-creation gets to go next.

39. *Tic-Tac-Toe.* You don't need paper and pencil for this old game if you've thought to use a permanent marker to draw a tic-tac-toe board on the bottom of a foamlite sleeping pad. Use rocks against sticks, or leaves, or whatever.

40. *Name that Tune.* One family member hums or whistles a song. The first person to name the tune becomes the hummer or whistler. If you prefer to have a "winner," it's the player who guesses the most songs correctly.

41. *Gossip.* One player whispers a made-up secret piece of "gossip" to a second player, who then passes it to a third player, and so on until the gossip returns to the player who started. The fun is seeing how much the information changes as it passes around the group. The larger the group, the greater the fun.

42. *Rocks-in-the-Jug.* If you have an empty plastic container, such as a milk jug, gather small rocks and take turns kneeling or standing over the jug and trying

to drop the rocks through the opening. For younger kids, cut the top off the jug to make the opening larger.

43. *Rocks-in-the-Jug, Part II.* Blindfold the player dropping the rocks and have a second player direct the drops.

44. *Hot Potato.* Stuff a sock with another sock or two, or perhaps a bandanna, and you've got the "hot potato." One player turns his or her back and begins to sing a tune. Any song will do. The rest of the family tosses the hot potato around the tent, holding onto it as briefly as possible. The singer stops singing whenever the urge strikes. The person holding the potato, or the last person to touch it, gets "burned" and becomes the singer. *Note: campers in nearby tents may ask you to be quieter.*

45. *World at Your Feet.* If your tent has a vestibule, gather around near the door and see how many different items you can find under the vestibule. Digging is allowed, and everything provides a chance to learn. Look for rocks and twigs, growing plants and dead plants, litter, worms, insects, and leaves. For added interest, "seed" the area first with treasures such as coins.

46. *The Ears Have It.* Everyone lies quietly and listens. Identify as many sounds as you can. The patter of rain. The gurgle of a nearby stream. Wind. Birdsong. Squirrel chatter.

47. *Rolling Stones.* This is a math game in which you find three or four small rocks approximately the same size but otherwise distinctly different. Assign a value to each stone starting at one. The black stone, for example, scores one; the reddish stone scores two, etc. Place them in a cup. Each player rolls the stones and scores the value of the stone that rolls farthest. Keep score. The first player to reach ten or fifty or a hundred wins.

48. *Rock, Paper, Scissors.* A *rock* is represented by your closed first, *paper* by your hand held flat, and *scissors* by extending the first two fingers of your hand (like the two blades of a pair of scissors). Players tap one hand on the palm of the other hand three times, and on the third tap make their playing hand into either rock, paper, or scissors. Scissors "cut" paper, and so scissors beat paper. Paper "covers" rock, so paper beats rock. Rock "breaks" scissors, so rock beats scissors. Two people play each other, and the loser is out until the next round. If the two players show the same hand, it's a tie and they play again. The winner plays the next person until only one overall winner remains. The overall winner gets the last cookie, piece of candy, and so on.

49. *Cat's Cradle.* For ages, manipulating pieces of string into unusual designs has fascinated young and old. Cat's cradle is probably the most well-known version of this activity. Buy the *Klutz Cat's Cradle* book for numerous easy-to-follow instructions. If you forget the string, tie your bootlaces or shoelaces together.

50. *Playing in the Rain.* Put on raingear. Lace up boots. Being tentbound is often more an attitude than a state of being. Kids don't melt in the rain. Neither will you.

APPENDIX D

CAMPING CHECKLIST

Use this checklist as a starting point, adding or subtracting items to meet your needs and wants:

The Tent
- ❏ tent
- ❏ fly
- ❏ poles
- ❏ stakes
- ❏ cord (for taut lines, clothesline, emergencies)
- ❏ tarp
- ❏ ground cloth

The Bedroom
- ❏ sleeping bags
- ❏ sleeping pads
- ❏ pillows
- ❏ blankets
- ❏ cots

The Kitchen
- ❏ food
- ❏ spices
- ❏ cooler
- ❏ ice
- ❏ stove
- ❏ fuel
- ❏ funnel
- ❏ matches/lighters
- ❏ pots
- ❏ potgrips
- ❏ pans
- ❏ lids
- ❏ coffeepot
- ❏ Dutch oven
- ❏ griddle

- [ ] camping oven
- [ ] tin foil
- [ ] spatula
- [ ] large spoon
- [ ] ladle
- [ ] kitchen knife
- [ ] cups
- [ ] plates
- [ ] bowls
- [ ] spoons
- [ ] forks
- [ ] dinner knives
- [ ] can opener
- [ ] corkscrew
- [ ] large plastic tub (for washing)
- [ ] dish soap
- [ ] scrubbing sponge
- [ ] paper towels
- [ ] drinking water
- [ ] water carrier
- [ ] beverage jug
- [ ] trash bags
- [ ] tablecloth

The Bathroom

- [ ] toilet paper
- [ ] towel
- [ ] soap
- [ ] shampoo
- [ ] comb
- [ ] brush
- [ ] toothbrush
- [ ] toothpaste
- [ ] large plastic tub (for washing)

The Closet

- [ ] hat/cap
- [ ] underwear
- [ ] long underwear
- [ ] jacket/sweater/vest
- [ ] pants (long)
- [ ] pants (short)
- [ ] swimsuit
- [ ] tee shirts
- [ ] long-sleeved shirts
- [ ] socks
- [ ] boots
- [ ] shoes
- [ ] gloves
- [ ] raingear
- [ ] bandanna

Bits and Pieces

- [ ] camp table
- [ ] camp chairs
- [ ] first-aid kit
- [ ] insect repellent
- [ ] sunscreen
- [ ] sunglasses
- [ ] lantern
- [ ] fuel
- [ ] funnel
- [ ] flashlights
- [ ] extra batteries
- [ ] hatchet
- [ ] saw
- [ ] shovel
- [ ] repair kit

Fun Things

❏ books
❏ camera and film
❏ journal
❏ pens (for writing, colored for drawing)
❏ playing cards
❏ glue
❏ toys
❏ binoculars
❏ maps
❏ compass
❏ day pack
❏ canoe
❏ paddles
❏ personal flotation devices
❏ bike
❏ biking helmet
❏ fishing gear

APPENDIX E

RESOURCES

Books and Magazines

Backpacker Magazine. Rodale Press, 33 East Minor Street, Emmaus, PA 18098. 610-967-5171. *www.backpacker.com.* Not just for backpackers, and a great source of advice for campers. The annual buyer's guide is an excellent resource for gear and clothing.

Carey, Alice. *Parents' Guide to Hiking and Camping.* New York: W. W. Norton & Company, 1997. A great resource for families new to camping.

Getchell, Annie. *The Essential Outdoor Gear Manual: Equipment Care & Repair for Outdoorspeople.* Camden, ME: Ragged Mountain Press, 1995. How to make your gear last longer, and, if it's broken, how to fix it.

Grant, Gordon. *Canoeing.* New York: W. W. Norton & Company, 1997. A great resource for paddling novices and intermediates who want to know more.

Hostetter, Kristin. *Don't Forget the Duct Tape: Tips and Tricks for Repairing Outdoor Gear.* Seattle, WA: The Mountaineers Books, 2004. All about keeping gear functional.

Martin, James. *Digital Photography Outdoors.* Seattle, WA: The Mountaineers Books, 2004. How to work more efficiently and creatively with a digital camera.

McGivney, Annette. *Leave No Trace: A Guide to the New Wilderness Etiquette.* Seattle, WA: The Mountaineers Books, 1998. How to use the land without causing harm.

Merwin, John. *Fly Fishing.* New York: W. W. Norton & Company, 1996. A great resource for the beginner.

NOLS. *Leave No Trace Master Educator Handbook.* Lander, WY: National Outdoor Leadership School, 2003. Step-by-step guide to teaching others about Leave No Trace.

Oliver, Peter. *Bicycling: Touring and Mountain Bike Basics.* New York: W. W. Norton & Company, 1995. A great resource for novices and intermediate bikers.

Politano, Colleen. *Lost in the Woods: Child Survival for Parents and Teachers.* Merrillville, IN: ICS Books, 1993 (distributed by Globe Pequot Press, Guilford, CT). How to teach kids to take care of themselves outdoors.

Prater, Yvonne, and Ruth Dyar Mendenhall (with Kerry Smith). *Beyond Gorp: Favorite Foods from Outdoor Experts.* Seattle, WA: The Mountaineers Books, 2005. A batch of tasty recipes contributed by many outdoor experts.

Tilton, Buck. *Backcountry First Aid & Extended Care.* Guilford, CT: Globe Pequot Press, 2002. How to recognize, treat, and prevent common outdoor emergencies.

Tilton, Buck. *Don't Get Bitten: The Dangers of Things that Bite or Sting.* Seattle, WA: The Mountaineers Books, 2003. How to avoid and, if that fails, treat bites and stings.

Tilton, Buck. *Don't Get Sick: The Hidden Dangers of Camping and Hiking.* Seattle, WA: The Mountaineers Books, 2002. How to prevent illness on camping trips.

Gear

Campmor, *www.campmor.com.* A complete shopping destination.

Cascade Designs, *www.cascadedesigns.com.* Therm-a-Rest pads.

Coleman Company, *www.coleman.com.* All you need—or just want.

Eureka! *www.eurekatent.com.* A complete line of tents and sleeping bags.

GSI Outdoors, *www.gsioutdoors.com.* The basics and the ultimate for the camping kitchen.

Jack Wolfskin, *www.jack-wolfskin.com.* Child carriers and more.

Katadyn Products, Inc., *www.katadyn.com.* Filters and halogens to disinfect water.

L. L. Bean, *www.llbean.com.* From A to Z in camping gear.

Nalgene, *www.nalgene-outdoors.com.* Screwtop containers, from small to large, including great water bottles.

Recreation Equipment, Inc., *www.rei.com.* Everything.

Who's Shoes, *www.whosshoesid.com.* Kids ID Kit, a small strap with personal information that attaches to shoestrings via a Velcro closure.

Wisconsin Pharmacal Company, *www.pharmacalway.com.* Atwater Cary first-aid kits—plus a medicine chest of outdoor health and safety products.

Maps

National Geographic Maps (*Trails Illustrated* enhanced topographic maps), P.O. Box 4357, Evergreen, CO 80437. 800-962-1643. *http://maps.nationalgeographic.com/trails.*

U.S. Geological Survey (USGS) Information Services (topographic maps), P.O. Box 25287, Denver, CO 80225. 888-275-8747. *http://ask.usgs.gov.*

Agencies

Bureau of Land management, *www.blm.gov.* Administers more than 260 million acres of public land, primarily in the eleven western states and Alaska.

National Park Service, *www.nps.gov* and *www.us-national-parks.net.* Administers more than 360 sites on public land.

National Park Society, *www.nationalparksociety.com.* To obtain *National Park Service Camping Guide.* Nonprofit organization helps you find your way through national parks.

ReserveAmerica, *www.reserveamerica.com.* One-stop shopping for campgrounds.

U.S. Fish & Wildlife Service, *www.fws.gov.* Administers approximately 700 refuges for the protection of animals and plants.

U.S. Forest Service, *www.fs.fed.us.* To obtain *National Forest Campground and Recreation Directory.* Administers almost 200 million acres of forests and grasslands.

Volunteers-in-Parks, *www.nps.gov/volunteer.*

Organizations

National Outdoor Leadership School, 284 Lincoln Street, Lander, WY 82520. 800-710-NOLS. *www.nols.edu.*

The Leave No Trace Center for Outdoor Ethics, P.O. Box 997, Boulder, CO 80306. 800-332-4100. *www.LNT.org.*

Wilderness Medicine Institute of NOLS, 284 Lincoln Street, Lander, WY 82520. *http://wmi.nols.edu.*

PHOTO CREDITS

Photographs on pages 8, 54, 62, 154 courtesy of Big City Mountaineers
Photographs on pages 12, 20 (top two images), 56,76, 78, 80, 83, 101, 131,
  133, 134, 136, 146 courtesy of Johnson Outdoors, Inc.
Photographs on pages 20 (bottom image), 24, 25, 28, 29, 30, 47, 48, 50, 65,
  69, 94 courtesy of The Coleman Company, Inc.
Photographs on page 21, 23, 31, 130 courtesy of LL Bean
Photographs on pages 30, 34, 35, 36 courtesy of GSI Outdoors
Photographs on pages 49, 114 courtesy of Wisconsin Pharmacal Company LLC
Photographs on pages 57, 72, 126, 127, 139, 143 courtesy of National
  Park Service
Photograph on page 84 courtesy of *www.morguefile.com*
Photograph on page 88 by Jane Lee
Photograph on page 124 courtesy of USDA
Photograph on page 138 © Jiange Jingjie/Agency: *www.dreamstime.com*
Photograph on page 149 courtesy of Katadyn Products, Inc.

INDEX

Giardia, 148
griddle, 35
grilling, 101-03
ground cloth, 22

H
halogens, 148-49
handwashing, 70
hatchet, 51
headlamp, 51
heat, 79
heat exhaustion, 121
heat stroke, 121
heating of tent, 67
high-intensity camping, 15-16
hiking, 125-29, 132
holidays, 61
human waste, 151-52, 161
hydration, 79
hygiene, 70-71, 161
hypothermia, 121-22

I
infection, 118-19
insect bites, 114
insect repellents, 81
insulation, 26

J
journal, 47

K
kerosene stove, 31
kids. *See* children
kindling, 90-91
kitchen
    cleanup of, 37, 70, 72, 157
    cookware, 32-35
    organization of, 34
    setup for, 69-70, 150
    stove. *See* stove(s)
    utensils, 35-36, 71

L
lanterns, 49-51

latrine, 152
Leave No Trace, 159-62
liquid-fuel lantern, 50-51
liquid-fuel stoves, 30
lost children, 85-86
low-intensity camping, 15-16
lunch, 94, 97-99

M
map, 127, 130-31
meals, ready-to-eat, 112
mealtime planning, 93-94.
    See also food; recipes
meat
    Dutch oven cooking of, 106
    foil cooking of, 108-09
    grilling of, 102-03
medications, 48-49, 81
medium-intensity camping, 16
mountain bikes, 132-33
mummy sleep bag, 27

N
National Park Service, 56-58, 88
nature trails, 126, 128-29
nylon, 45

O
oak, 124
open-cell foam pads, 24

P
packing of vehicle, 52-53
paddling, 135-39
pans
    cooking with, 103-05
    description of, 32, 70-71
partial-dome tent, 21
peer pressure, 86
personal flotation device, 135
pets, 87-88

photography, 143-44
pillow, 28
pit vipers, 115
pitching of tent, 17-18, 66-67
poison ivy, 124
poisoning, 81
poles, 18-19
poncho, 44
portable toilet, 151-52
potgrips, 34
pots
    cooking with, 103-05
    description of, 32, 70-71
propane lantern, 50
propane stoves, 30-31

R
radiation, 41
recipes, 95-100, 104, 106-08. *See also* food
rectangular sleeping bag, 27
renting gear, 16
repair kits, 52
reservations, 64

S
safety, 14, 82, 142, 146-47
sanitization, 71
saw, 51
scorpion stings, 115
sealing seams, 22
seasons, 19
self-inflating mattresses, 23-24
semi-rectangular sleeping bag, 28
shovel, 51-52
shower, 153, 161
sleeping bags
    cleaning of, 156
    description of, 25
    dryness of, 27
    insulation of, 26
    preparation of, 68

ABOUT
THE AUTHORS

(Photo by Steve Smith/Backpacker)

Buck Tilton, a contributing editor to *Backpacker Magazine* since 1989, has been selecting sites and setting up camps for thirty-five years. He has more than 1000 magazine articles and 30 books to his credit. His books include *Don't Get Sick, Don't Get Bitten,* and *Trekker's Handbook,* all published by The Mountaineers Books. He lives in Lander, Wyoming, with his wife Kathleen.

Kristin Hostetter is *Backpacker Magazine's* Gear Editor. In addition to managing the magazine's gear coverage, she writes a column for the *Seattle Post-Intelligencer* and has authored two books: *Don't Forget The Duct Tape: Tips and Tricks for Repairing Outdoor Gear* and *Backpacker's Adventure Journal.* Kristin lives in Milton, Massachusetts, with her husband, Shaun, and her two boys, Charlie and Joe.

(Photo by Kit Noble)

THE MOUNTAINEERS, founded in 1906, is a nonprofit outdoor activity and conservation club, whose mission is "to explore, study, preserve, and enjoy the natural beauty of the outdoors. . . . " Based in Seattle, Washington, the club is now one of the largest such organizations in the United States, with seven branches throughout Washington State.

The Mountaineers sponsors both classes and year-round outdoor activities in the Pacific Northwest, which include hiking, mountain climbing, ski-touring, snow-shoeing, bicycling, camping, kayaking, nature study, sailing, and adventure travel. The club's conservation division supports environmental causes through educational activities, sponsoring legislation, and presenting informational programs.

All club activities are led by skilled, experienced instructors, who are dedicated to promoting safe and responsible enjoyment and preservation of the outdoors.

If you would like to participate in these organized outdoor activities or the club's programs, consider a membership in The Mountaineers. For information and an application, write or call The Mountaineers, Club Headquarters, 7700 Sand Point Way NE, Seattle, WA 98115; 206-521-6001. You can also visit the club's website at www.mountaineers.org or contact The Mountaineers via email at clubmail@mountaineers.org.

The Mountaineers Books, an active, nonprofit publishing program of the club, produces guidebooks, instructional texts, historical works, natural history guides, and works on environmental conservation. All books produced by The Mountaineers Books fulfill the club's mission.

Send or call for our catalog of more than 500 outdoor titles:

The Mountaineers Books
1001 SW Klickitat Way, Suite 201
Seattle, WA 98134
800-553-4453
mbooks@mountaineersbooks.org
www.mountaineersbooks.org

The Mountaineers Books is proud to be a corporate sponsor of The Leave No Trace Center for Outdoor Ethics, whose mission is to promote and in-spire responsible outdoor recreation through education, research, and part-nerships. The Leave No Trace program is focused specifically on human-powered (nonmotorized) recreation.

Leave No Trace strives to educate visitors about the nature of their recreational impacts, as well as offer techniques to prevent and minimize such impacts. Leave No Trace is best understood as an educational and ethical program, not as a set of rules and regulations.

For more information, visit *www.LNT.org,* or call 800-332-4100.

OTHER TITLES YOU MIGHT ENJOY FROM
THE MOUNTAINEERS BOOKS

Day Hiker's Handbook: Get Started with the Experts
Michael Lanza
Learn how to get started on the trails, what gear to choose, how to handle dangers, and much more.

Everyday Wisdom: 1001 Expert Tips for Hikers
Karen Berger
Expert tips and tricks for hikers and backpackers selected from a popular *Backpacker* magazine column.

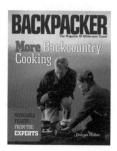

More Backcountry Cooking: Moveable Feasts from the Experts
Dorcas Miller
Practical, tasty recipes that are quick, easy, and nutritious.

Don't Get Bitten: The Dangers of Things that Bite or Sting
Buck Tilton
Don't Get Eaten: The Dangers of Animals that Charge or Attack
Dave Smith
From bugs and snakes to bears and cougars, these handy pocket guides explain eveything you need to know to stay safe in the woods.

BEST HIKES WITH DOGS SERIES

No one loves the forest more than the family dog! This guidebook series provides trails selected specifically for hiking with a four-legged friend, as well as information on keeping your dog safe on the trail.

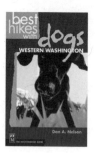

Available at fine bookstores and outdoor stores, by phone at 800-553-4453 or on the web at *www.mountaineersbooks.org*

THE MOUNTAINEERS BOOKS